Introduction to Databases: A Focus on Practical Solutions

David C. Roberts

First Edition

Jada Press, Potomac, Maryland

First Edition

ISBN 979-8-9855085-0-5

Printed in the United States of America.

Preface

This book is intended for a one-semester first graduate computer science course on database management systems or an upper-division computer science undergraduate course.

Relational database management systems provide on-line access to huge collections of data, with simultaneous access by large numbers of users and processes, while assuring the correctness of data and protecting it from machine and software malfunctions and even complete loss of the database. These systems today provide the foundation for systems that process large numbers of transactions continually, that must preserve correct data.

Developing applications that access data stored by these systems plays an important role for computer science graduates, and it will continue to be important as long as large online transaction processing applications are in use. This book is intended as a course for programmers who will build applications that use these systems. It is used for a first computer science graduate course in database management systems.

Most database management texts for use at the graduate level are written by researchers in universities. Over years of working with programmers who have graduate degrees in computer science, I have learned that these books,

4

and the courses taught from them, do not prepare students adequately for competent application development work. This text emphasizes three topics that my experience indicates that working programmers commonly do not understand well:

1. Data independence,
2. normalization and
3. data modeling.

In addition, application programmers often don't understand how database systems work, so when they experience problems with their applications, particularly performance problems, they are not well-equipped to solve them.

Part I of the book covers the skills to develop database applications: the relational data language SQL, normalization and data modeling.

Part II provides an overview of how database systems work, so that practitioners can understand how problems can develop and where to look for solutions.

Finally, the use of theory and mathematical notation in this text differs from others. The approach used here has been called "just in time, just enough" math and theory. Thus, enough theory is presented so that each topic is covered completely and correctly. However, superfluous theory and proofs that have no practical consequences are not included.

Because of the "just in time, just enough" approach, transaction scheduling is covered, although it is usually found only in more advanced books, as is the ARIES algorithm for recovery, which is used by all widely used database systems today. In addition, fourth normal form, often omitted from textbooks as being of only academic interest, is included, because it is needed in practical situations, and can be addressed without pages and pages of theory.

Acknowledgement

Thanks to Rahul Simha for convincing me that computer science textbooks use too much math and introducing me to his concept of "just enough math" to understand the subject. His ideas helped me solidify my own thinking on the subject, and form the approach used in this book.

Thanks to my wife Mary Jane, who had considerably less companionship during the pandemic while the book was being written.

Thanks to Herb Edelstein and Dave Grossman for encouraging me to write the book when I doubted my ability to complete it. Thanks to Steve Kaisler for practical advice on many aspects of book publication.

Finally, thanks to my many database students through the years since 1975, when I started teaching the subject, who have challenged my ideas and helped me refine my thinking and teaching methods.

6

Table of Contents

10

I.   Database Applications

Part I introduces the basic tools for developing database applications:

> the unified data language SQL, for defining, accessing, changing, and controlling the database.

> normalization, the theory of database structure, that guides the design of the database, reducing programming complexity.

> data modeling, the methods used to design the database structure.

SQL is used by every major relational database system and is the subject of an international standard. Therefore, with some product-to-product variations, the language is similar for all major database systems. The SQL examples in the book follow the standard, with some departures that follow Oracle's version of SQL, because Oracle has the leading market share of database systems.

Normalization is a body of theory developed to guide the design of database structure; normalization theory provides a method to determine which structure for a database will avoid problems. In my experience working with professional programmers who have taken graduate courses in database management, they typically do not understand how to apply normalization. The approach used here was developed to solve this problem, by providing a method for understanding normalization theory and realizing its importance.

The approach taken to normalization theory in this book is to first focus on a set of plain English rules for database design that, when followed, produce a highly normalized database. Using these rules as a framework, the theory is presented, so that the practical application and consequences of the theory are easy to understand.

The Entity-Relation method of data modeling is widely used. The concepts of the E-R approach as introduced by Chen, with lots of examples and categorization of types of relationships by cardinality, are presented here.

Data modeling is best learned not by reading about it or doing it by yourself, but by doing it and talking to colleagues about it. Several data modeling exercises have been included, so that a different problem can be assigned to every one or two students. Students can each develop a data model, then bring their model to class and present it to the rest of the class. Those discussions tend to reveal alternative approaches, reinforcing the lessons of the book.

On-Line Analytical Processing, OLAP, uses data provided by a transaction processing DBMS to perform analyses of historical data. There may be a separate database system for the OLAP task, or the transaction processing DBMS may incorporate OLAP features, so that both OLAP and transaction processing can be performed using the same database.

The specialized data models used for OLAP are explored, along with the processing algorithm that permits rapid processing of the large tables that are typically found.

Chapter 1   Introduction

1.1   What Is a Database System?

Wikipedia defines a database as an organized collection of data, usually stored and accessed electronically using a computer system. The collection of data could be an organization's business data, covering such areas as employees, customers, buildings, inventory, orders and others. It could be a library's holdings, such as books, magazines, audio recordings, videos and more. Or it could be any other collection of information.

A database management system is the software that tends the database, in every way:

- It interacts with end-users, with applications, and with the database itself.
- It captures data entered into the database,
- It performs updates requested by end users and applications,
- It maintains the correctness of data by enforcing integrity constraints,
- It allows hundreds or thousands of programs and users to interact with the database at the same time, and
- in case of a failure of computer hardware or software, it ensures that the contents of the database remain correct and usable.

An analogy to a database system is a magic filing cabinet. Imagine the sort of file cabinet you see in the office every day but given some new features through magic. Somehow, this magic filing cabinet allows hundreds or thousands of people to all browse through the files at the same time, without ever interfering with each other. These people can even make changes to information stored in the files, and they still don't interfere with each other or cause any errors. While all these people are making changes, the magic file cabinet also checks all the cross-references between the various files that they are changing, preventing any changes that would cause incorrect cross-references. Finally, if the file cabinet catches fire, or the whole office building collapses, the magic file cabinet somehow reconstitutes itself so that all the files are present exactly as they were before the disaster and are ready for use again.

1.2   Data Independence

A basic goal set by Ted Codd in the first paper that described the relational approach[1] for the relational approach was to allow information stored in large databases to "be accessed without knowing how the information was structured or where it resided in the database."[2] Before relational databases, programs to process data such as bank accounts, credit cards, stock trading, and travel reservations, to give just a few examples, were complex to write because the

---

[1] Edgar F. Codd. A Relational Model of Data for Large Shared Data Banks. *Communications of the ACM* 13,6 (June 1970), 377-387.

[2] IBM 100.   Icons of Progress: Relational Database. https://www.ibm.com/ibm/history/ibm100/us/en/icons/reldb/

programs had to deal with the physical structure of the files as they were stored. Today, such programs reference an abstract model of the data, based on relational theory.

The programmer deals with a simple, tabular view of data. That simple view is distinct from how the data is stored. Many adjustments can be made in the storage arrangement, to meet performance requirements, without changing the programmer's view of data.

Jim Gray, a participant in the original IBM Research project on relational database said that Codd's "relational data model was at first very controversial; people thought that the model was too simplistic and that it could never give good performance."[3] Early relational database systems did not provide a lot of flexibility in how data was stored—the physical structure of the database looked very much like relational tables. The term "table as file" describes this early approach. Today's relational systems offer much greater flexibility in the physical structure of the database, an important factor in achieving high performance.

1.3   Concurrency
The method used to permit many processes to change a database at the same time is central to the use of

---

[3] Computer Science: Reflections on the Field, Reflections from the Field. National Research Council, Division on Engineering and Physical Sciences, Computer Science and Telecommunications Board, Committee on the Fundamentals.

database systems.   Without concurrent access by many processes, only one process or user could access the database system at a time.   Most modern applications, such as online banking, could not exist.

When you write a program to access data in a database, the DBMS will handle concurrency issues for you.   If you understand how this service is provided, you will be able to write your programs so that they don't limit concurrency.

Some of the problems that can occur with concurrency are shown below.   These and others are discussed in more detail in Chapter 7.

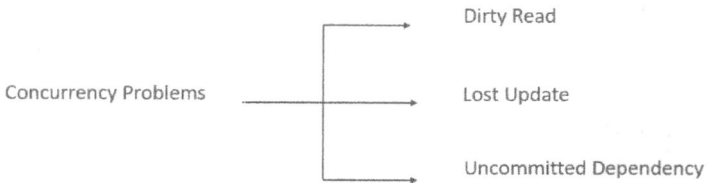

```
                                                    Dirty Read

                            ┌──────────▶
Concurrency Problems  ──────┤──────────▶          Lost Update

                            └──────────▶
                                                    Uncommitted Dependency
```

1.4   Recovery

As you know, computers today are reliable.   For example, a disk drive typically lasts for years before failing.   Although an individual might simply assume the risk of failure when using a personal computer, a bank can't afford to lose all its account data because a disk drive fails or there is a software problem.   In the event of a failure, there must be a way to recover data.   However, the overhead introduced by recovery processes must be limited, so that performance requirements can be met.

The types of failures that require recovery are storage device failures, software failures and failures of a transaction. These are discussed in Chapter 7.

Here, too, understanding how recovery works can help you provide for recovery in your own programs.

1.5   Integrity

There are three important areas where database systems can help maintain the integrity of stored data.

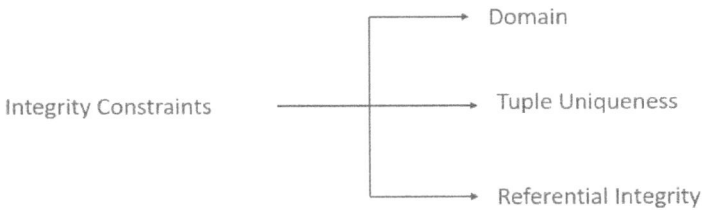

```
                                          ──→  Domain

Integrity Constraints  ─────────────┤    ──→  Tuple Uniqueness

                                          ──→  Referential Integrity
```

First is domain integrity. You can specify that the values entered in one column of the table must be members of a specified set of values. In our employee example, you might require that each job title be one of a list of established job titles for the company.

Another is referential integrity. You can require that the department number shown for each employee is the number of an actual department. That's a reasonable constraint; consider for a moment what could happen if an employee was shown assigned to a nonexistent department number. A report of total salary by department wouldn't include that employee's salary in the salaries of any department. Thus, the total salaries for the entire company would be greater than the total of the salaries of all departments. Referential constraints allow you to establish a constraint that a value in one table must be an identifying value in another table.

Entity integrity is the third, that allows you to require that each instance of an entity described in the database must have a unique identifier. An example would be the use of a generated employee number or the social security number for each employee as a unique identifier. This is illustrated below:

Entity Integrity

CUSTOMERS

Cust#	Cust_Name	City	State
98	ABC Co.	Denver	CO
47	DEF Co.	Chicago	IL
876	GHI Co.	Provo	UT

Referential Integrity   Domain Integrity

ORDERS

Order#	Cust#	Date	Date_Shipped
34	876	6/15/2021	6/8/2021
35	47	6/16/2021	6/19/2021
36	876	6/16/2021	6/18/2021
37	98	6/17/2020	

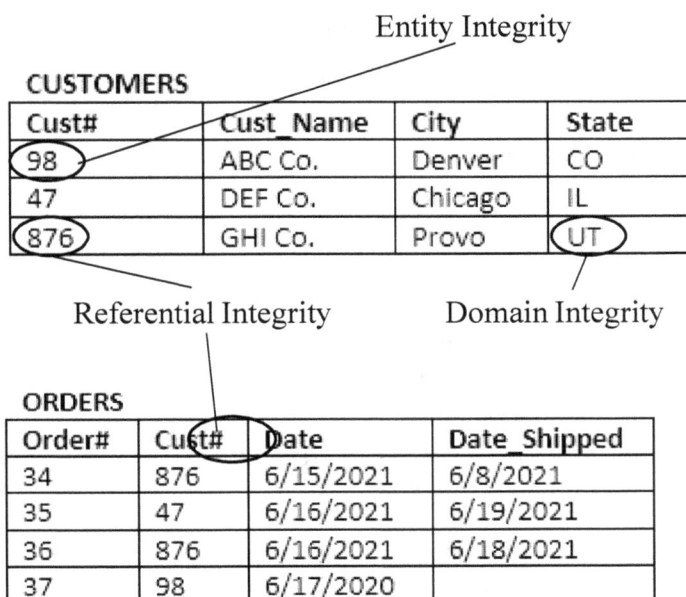

Figure 1. Integrity Constraints

1.6   Relational Database

Ted Codd, a mathematician who worked at IBM research, is the inventor of the relational approach.[4] He was concerned that there was little theory considering the storage and use of data. He thought that underpinning work in data with theory could make that work much more effective. He also wanted to establish a theory that would allow us to identify which database designs, also called data models, were most appropriate.

---

[4] Codd, Edgar.F., A relational model of data for large shared data banks, *Communications of the ACM* 13, 6 (Jun. 1970), 377-387.

Some theory around relational database is not of practical significance to programmers who are developing applications that use relational database systems; the coverage of relational theory in this book is limited to the theory that is useful for building applications.

One part of that theory has considerable practical importance but is not well understood by many programmers who work with relational databases: normalization theory. A practical approach to normalize a database is presented first, and then that approach is used as a framework to introduce normalization theory.

A relational database is a set of relations. The notion of *relation* comes from discrete mathematics, not referring to relation*ships* that are represented in the database. In practical terms, each relation looks like a table of data—in fact, they are also called tables, the term used in this book. The database is concerned with entities, which are the things that are the subjects of data, and attributes of entities, which are the characteristics of those things. Thus, each table is comprised of data about one type of entity; each row in the table contains data about a single instance of that entity type.

Consider this example of a simple relational database:

CUSTOMERS

Cust#	Cust_Name	City	State
98	ABC Co.	Denver	CO
47	DEF Co.	Chicago	IL
876	GHI Co.	Provo	UT

ORDERS

Order#	Cust#	Date	Date_Shipped
34	876	6/15/2021	6/8/2021
35	47	6/16/2021	6/19/2021
36	876	6/16/2021	6/18/2021
37	98	6/17/2020	

This database consists of two tables, so it describes two entity types, customers and orders. Each entity type has four attributes. A customer has a customer number assigned, that the company uses internally. Of course, there's the customer's name and the city and state where the customer is located. Each order has an order number, as well as the customer number of the customer who placed the order. The date the order was placed is recorded, along with the date the order was shipped.

Keep in mind that these two tables are a programming abstraction that an application program uses to access data. The data may or may not be organized this way in the database.

1.7   Data Models

A data model organizes data elements for a database and provides a standardized way to represent how the data elements relate to each other.[5] Because the data represents the properties of real things, such as people, places and things and the events that connect them, the data model is a representation of reality.

The data model determines the final structure of the database, that is, the tables and columns that comprise it.

An entity-relation diagram (ERD) is commonly used to represent a data model. The ERD shows entity types, attributes, and relationships among entity types. The figure below shows an ERD for the example of customers and orders:

---

[5] Princeton University Center for Data Analytics & Reporting, Princeton, N.J.   2021.   *What is a Data Model?* https://cedar.princeton.edu/understanding-data/what-data-model

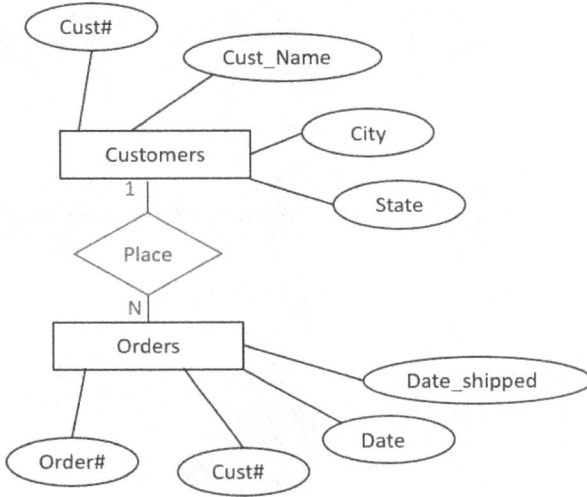

Figure 2. Data Model: Customers and Orders

In this diagram, the two entity types, each depicted by a rectangle, depict the two tables. The diamond between customers and orders gives a name to the relationship, that customers *place* orders, and shows that for each customer there may be zero or more orders (indicated by the *N*), and for each order there must be exactly one customer (indicated by the *1*).

This diagram is also called a Chen diagram after its inventor, Peter Chen.[6] Data modeling is the topic of Chapter 4.

---

[6] Chen, Peter, The entity-relationship model—toward a unified view of data. *ACM Transactions on Database Systems*, 1, 1 (Mar. 1976), 9-36.

1.8   Normalization

The data model is designed at the outset of an application project when the project team is beginning to learn about the data and the processes that act on it. Unfortunately, errors in designing the data model can have significant impact on the difficulty (hence cost and time required) of an application project. Unfortunately, crucial decisions that are based on an understanding of the data, that will have major impact on the project, must be made when the data is least understood.

Thanks to the search for criteria for sound data models carried out by Ted Codd and others, we have rules for what constitutes a sound data model that will not require major changes during software development. These criteria make up normalization theory.

In this book, data modeling is approached first through a set of simple English rules that, when followed, yield a high-quality data model. Then, normalization theory is introduced and its parallels to the plain English rules are explored. The goal is to provide the reader with an intuitive understanding of how to develop a data model, but also to be able to communicate with those who use the theory. Normalization is the topic of Chapter 3.

1.9   Data Language

As part of a research project into relational database described in a 1976 paper[7], IBM developed the data language, now called SQL. This data language, along with the other IBM-developed relational technology, is employed by most commercial relational database systems today.

SQL is a declarative language, that you use to specific a desired result. The database system then has the job of figuring out how to deliver the specified result.

SQL can be used interactively as well as through an application program. This single language is used to define the structure of the database, including integrity constraints, to retrieve from the database, to change values stored in the database, and to control access to the database.

Here are two examples of SQL statements to retrieve data from the database:

---

[7] Chamberlin, D. D., et. Al. SEQUEL 2: A unified approach to data definition, manipulation, and control. *IBM Journal of Research and Development* (Nov. 1976), 560-575.

```
SELECT *
FROM EMP
WHERE SAL >= 10000;
```

```
SELECT ENAME
FROM EMP
WHERE SAL >= (SELECT AVG(SAL) FROM EMP);
```

The first statement retrieves the entire row for each employee with a salary of more than 10,000. The second retrieves the names of employees who earn more than the average salary of all employees. The second select statement uses nesting; the innermost query computes the average salary, and the outermost query compares that to the salary of each employee. SQL is the subject of Chapter 2.

Chapter 2   Relational Data Languages

The relational data model was first introduced by Edgar F Codd, revealed to the world in a paper published in the Communications of the ACM in 1970.[8] The relational model organizes a database as a collection of independent tables. Don Chamberlin, a colleague of Codd's, said that his "basic idea was that relationships between data items should be based on the item's values, and not on separately specified linking or nesting. This notion greatly simplified the specification of queries and allowed unprecedented flexibility to exploit existing data sets in new ways."[9]

The origin of the term *relational* comes from the term *relation* in discrete mathematics. Ted Codd showed that a tabular structure of data could be represented as a mathematical relation. His intent was to introduce a theoretical basis to the way data was organized. However, that theory doesn't influence how relational databases are used in practice, so it is omitted from this book. The relevant theory is normalization theory, the topic of Chapter 3.

Ted Codd was well-rewarded for his pioneering work. In 1976, IBM made him an IBM fellow, providing a $100,000 salary, along with the freedom

---

[8] Edgar F. Codd, Ibid.
[9] IBM, *ibid.*

for life to work on any problem of his choosing, with research support provided by IBM. The ACM further honored Dr. Codd with its most important award for pioneering innovation, the Turing award, in 1981.[10] Nevertheless, he was disappointed with the relational products that IBM introduced, and he resigned his position as an IBM fellow.

All major database system products today use the relational approach. Every day, all over the world, this technology makes databases accessible for update by many independent processes at once, preventing them from interfering with one another, and providing recovery from hardware and software errors and even complete loss of the database. Relational database systems are the foundation of online systems for banks and for a great variety of major businesses.

Oracle was the first company to aggressively market a commercial relational database product, based on IBM's system R experimental system. In the early 1970s, IBM developed system R and installed it as an experiment at several customer sites. When the experiment ended, the researchers wrote several papers on the design of system R, the SQL data language, and the very positive reception the system received by the customers who had a chance

---

[10] C. J. Date, Edgar F. Codd. Association for Computing Machinery, 1981 A.M. Turing Award.

to use it. The founders of Oracle brought their product to market based on the outlines of the System R project in 1979.

Later, when IBM developed and introduced their production relational database systems, they further refined many of the algorithms employed. They published papers on this work as well. Virtually all of today's important relational systems incorporate elements of that IBM work.

Because of that common genesis of the major systems, it is possible to identify some basic algorithms for relational database management, presented in this book, and while they do not exactly describe any specific system, they are close to what is implemented by every major system.

2.1   Tables

A relational database stores information as a collection of independent tables.   Each table describes all the instances of some entity type that is of interest.   For example, in the table shown below, employees are the entity type that is described.

EMP

EMPNO	ENAME	DEPTNO	JOB	MGR	SAL	COMM
20	SMITH	3	PRES		150	
30	CHEN	3	VPRES	20	120	
40	LIU	5	SALES MGR	30	100	
50	JONES	5	SALES REP	40	20	50

Figure 3. Employee Table

Each row of the table stores information about a single instance of that entity type. In the example table, each row of the table stores information about a single employee.

A table can also be called by its more formal name, a relation, and a row can be called a tuple. Those terms refer to exactly what we will call a table and a row.

The database is a model, in data, of some process or situation in the world outside the computer. The structure of the entire database, therefore, is called the *data model*. Designing the data model is simply identifying the entity types and their attributes that are to be included in the database. Data modeling is the subject of Chapter 4.

A definition of all the tables and other structures of a database is also called the *schema*, which includes:

> Tables
> Relationships
> Constraints
> Stored functions and procedures
> Views
> Indexes

2.2   Relational Algebra

The first relational data language, designed by Ted Codd, was relational algebra. He was interested in a data language with formal elegance; indeed, this language has only five commands and he proved that it can derive from a relational database any result that is consistent with the contents of the database. However, relational algebra is procedural, so it requires the user to write a procedure of set-theoretic commands to derive any result from the database, a potentially complex task.

Relational algebra is not used by any important commercial database system, but because it's part of the language used by database professionals, it's given a brief introduction here.

Relational algebra has just these five commands:

- Select—choose a subset of rows that make some proposition true

- Project—choose a subset of columns

- Product—each row of one table appended to each row of second table

- Set Union—all the rows of two tables (tables must have similar columns)

- Set Difference—the rows of one table with some removed that appear in another table (with similar columns)

The following sequence of statements in relational algebra will produce a list of employee names and the location where they work.

SELECT (EMP X DEPT) WHERE EMP.DEPTNO
= DEPT.DEPTNO

PROJECT ON EMP.ENAME, DEPT.LOC

The product operation inside the parentheses pastes together every row of EMP with every row of DEPT. If EMP has *m* rows and DEPT has *n* rows, this result will have *mn* rows. The SELECT operator, applied to this structure, chooses the compound rows that have equal values for DEPTNO. That is, every row from EMP is paired with the row from DEPT that has a matching value for DEPTNO. The PROJECT command then removes all but ENAME and LOC from the combined row, giving the desired result.

As you can see, for a non-programmer, relational algebra sequences are not easy to write or to read. It is not in use by any important database system today.

2.3   SQL

SQL is the data language in use by all important relational database systems today.

The System R team called their data language Sequel, an acronym for Structured English Query Language.   Later, when IBM introduced a commercial relational database product, they discovered that another company had already trademarked the name Sequel, so IBM renamed the language SQL.

SQL offers these principal advantages:

- accessing many records with a single command.

- It does not specify how to carry out an operation.

- It uses a human-readable syntax that is quickly understood and usable.

- It provides a single language for all database functions: definition, access control

SQL has been standardized, so there is basic similarity of the language across different database platforms.

DBMS Functions

These are the functions of a database system. SQL is a unified language that is used for all of them.

Data definition—names, structure, format of data

manipulation—CRUD (create, retrieve, update, delete)

administration—control access

control—specify user privileges.

SQL can be used interactively, or it can be used from a program. When it's used from a program, the program passes a SQL statement to the database system, then gets back the result one row at a time.

Bag Language

Relational algebra is said to be a relational language, because the result of any relational algebra operation is a relation. That is not strictly true for SQL. Although the result of a SQL query looks like a table, there is one difference that keeps SQL from being truly a relational language: the result of a SELECT statement is not a table, which would have unique rows, but what is called a *bag*. A bag is like a set except that it can have duplicate entries. Thus, if the result was a table, it wouldn't have duplicates, but since it's a bag, it can have duplicates.

Consider this of our example database

SELECT DEPTNO FROM EMP;

would produce this result:

DEPTNO
3
3
5
5

The designers of SQL made this decision because if every result of a SELECT statement required that duplicates be eliminated from every result, often requiring considerable extra processing, even when duplicates were not a possible result. Instead, they provided the term DISTINCT to specify that duplicates were to be eliminated.

SELECT DISTINCT DEPTNO FROM EMP;

<u>DEPTNO</u>

3

5

2.4 Tables in SQL

A relational database is stored as a set of tables, and SQL is used to define the results of an operation to be performed. The only data structures referenced in a SQL statement are the values of data stored in rows and columns. This figure shows some basic concepts:

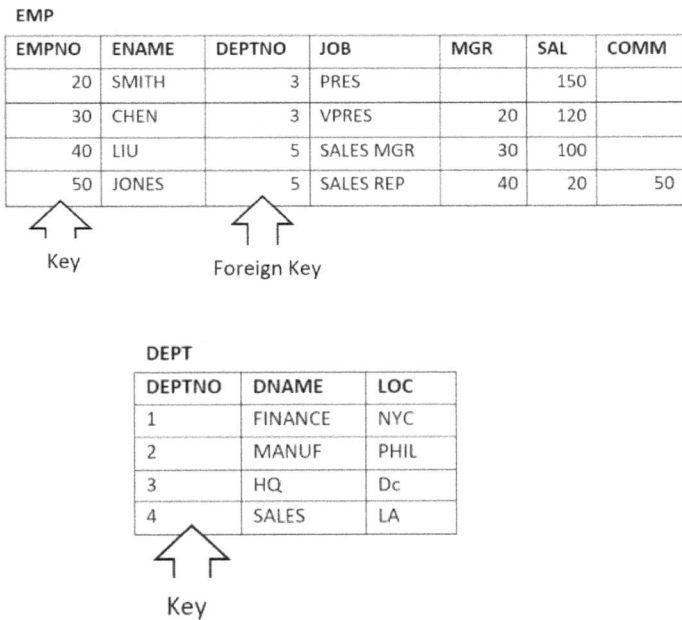

EMP

EMPNO	ENAME	DEPTNO	JOB	MGR	SAL	COMM
20	SMITH	3	PRES		150	
30	CHEN	3	VPRES	20	120	
40	LIU	5	SALES MGR	30	100	
50	JONES	5	SALES REP	40	20	50

Key   Foreign Key

DEPT

DEPTNO	DNAME	LOC
1	FINANCE	NYC
2	MANUF	PHIL
3	HQ	Dc
4	SALES	LA

Key

Figure 4. Tables, Keys, Foreign Keys

Recall that each table describes the instances of a particular entity type—that is, something that's a subject of data in the database. In this example, the entity types are employees and departments. Each row of the employee table corresponds to a single instance of the entity type employee: that is, a single employee. Similarly, each row of the department table corresponds to an instance of the entity type department: that is, a single department.

Because a row describes an instance of an entity, such as an employee, each row must be unique. In the case of an employee, for example, if a row is duplicated, then the same employee appears twice in the database. Does that employee get two paychecks? Does that employee count as two employees?

Because each row must be unique, there must be a single column or a combination of columns that uniquely identify the rows. That is, the group of columns that makes the rows different from each other. In the case of employees, that might be a social security number or an employee number. In the example of Figure 4, an employee number has been assigned to use to identify employees in the database. EMPNO identifies rows in the table as well as employees in the real world. We call EMPNO the *key* for that table. Similarly, an identifier has been assigned to each department, and department number is the key for DEPT.

For data integrity, every employee must be shown as assigned to a department in the department table. Therefore, the column DEPTNO in the employee table has been designated a foreign key, which means that the value in that column must be a key in another table. The database enforces this requirement, preventing possible inconsistent data in the database.

Foreign key constraints are an important tool for data integrity. In fact, the first relational systems introduced by IBM did not have that constraint, and it was cited as one reason why Ted Codd resigned his position at IBM, even after being named an IBM Fellow.

2.5   Data Types in SQL

All the major database systems today have many data types. Data types allow the database to offer specialized computations without custom programming. For example, comparisons and arithmetic are very different for decimal numbers and dates; but because these are distinct data types, SQL deals with them in the same way. A multitude of data types reduces programming effort and avoids many runtime errors.

The data types provided by a database system differ from system to system. They can be divided into these categories:

1. Numbers: INT, FLOAT, REAL, BIGINT
2. Date and time: DATE, TIME, DATETIME
3. Character and strings: CHAR, VARCHAR, TEXT

4. Unicode character strings: NTEXT, NCHAR, NVARCHAR
5. Binary numbers: BINARY, VARBINARY
6. Others: CLOB, BLOB, XML

Because of the variation in database systems, the discussion in this book uses just a few data types:

- varchar(n): variable length string up to n characters long
- char(n):   fixed length string of n characters
- number(n.d): decimal number of n digits, d to the right of the decimal point

2.6   Form of a SQL Statement

Each SQL statement can be regarded as an imperative sentence about the operation to be carried out. The sentence starts with a verb that specifies the operation: SELECT, INSERT, UPDATE or DELETE.   Following the verb are the subject and predicate.   The subject is the tables to be acted on; the predicate specifies a combination of conditions that can be evaluated as true, false or unknown. Following the predicate, additional clauses can specify some other operations, such as GROUP BY and ORDER BY.

A SQL statement is intended as a specification of the result of the statement, and not as direction on how to carry out the operation. The method used to carry out the operation will depend on the physical structure of the database, not on the tabular structure referenced by an application.

2.7   Data Retrieval

The SELECT statement defines the result of a retrieval operation. It's the statement that is used most often and is the richest statement in the language.

Consider this SELECT statement:

```
SELECT ENAME
FROM EMP
WHERE SAL > 100;
```

This statement will retrieve all values of the ENAME column from the EMP table for rows that have a value of SAL greater than 100.

Note that this statement, although it specifies an operation to be carried out, does not specify how the operation is to be performed. The operation might be carried out by retrieving all the rows of EMP, comparing each value of SAL to 100. However, if there is an index on SAL, then the operation could be performed by scanning the index, retrieving only the rows with values of SAL over 100.

How a SQL statement is processed by the database system can depend on the physical structure of the database and the values of data.

This independence of the abstract structure seen by programs and the physical structure is called *data independence;* it's a central goal of the relational approach. The database is tuned for performance by changing its physical structure, without the need to change application programs.

Literals

Literals are explicit values in the SQL statement, that could be called *constants*. SQL provides test, numeric and datetime literals. A text literal in a SQL statement is surrounded by single quotes, as in:

'SMITH'

'SALES'

SQL is case-sensitive with string literals, so the string literal 'Smith' would not be found equal to 'SMITH'.

Numeric literals are written as integers, decimal numbers or in scientific notation, like the following:

100

3

33.55

Date literals use the Georgian calendar. A form of date literal that doesn't include a time portion is

DATE '2022-12-25'

Reserved Words

SQL has many reserved words. The names of the operations listed above are just some of them. These reserved words cannot be used as the names of tables, columns, or indexes. SQL is not case-sensitive with reserved words.

Identifiers

SQL is also case-insensitive with identifiers, so you can write them in upper or lower case as you please.

Comments

For complex SQL statements, comments can help you—or someone else—in case there's a need for some changes to your application. There are two forms of comments.

A single-line comment starts with two consecutive hyphens and allows you to use the rest of the line for comments, like this:

```
        SELECT *                --retrieve    all
columns
        FROM EMP                --from        the
EMP table
        WHERE SAL >= 120;              --with
salary over 120
```

A multiple-line comment starts with /* and ends with */, like the following example:

```
        /* delete rows for all employees who earn
        more than the average salary for all
        employees */
        DELETE FROM EMP
        WHERE SAL >
                (SELECT AVG(SAL) FROM EMP);
```

The syntax for SELECT on a single table is:

```
        SELECT <column>
```

FROM <table>
WHERE <predicate on rows>
GROUP BY <columns>
HAVING <predicate on groups>
ORDER BY <columns>
OFFSET
FETCH FIRST

The SELECT clause lists the column values to be retrieved. The FROM clause lists the tables that are involved in the query. WHERE is a predicate, which is a combination of conditions on values of columns. The WHERE clause is evaluated for each row, and the rows that make the WHERE clause true are returned by the SELECT statement. GROUP BY forms the retrieved rows into groups and HAVING gives conditions on which groups to retrieve. ORDER BY specifies the order of presentation of results.

OFFSET gives the number of rows to skip before returning the result, and FIRST limits the number of rows to be returned.

Case Sensitivity
SQL is case-insensitive for reserved words, table names and column names. Thus, SELECT, Select and select are treated identically, as are DEPT, Dept and dept.

However, literal strings are case-sensitive, so 'Seattle', 'SEATTLE' and 'seattle' are not treated as equal.

Note that * in the SELECT list stands for "all columns", so that

    SELECT *

    FROM EMP;

will list all the columns in all the rows in the EMP table.

WHERE Clause

Adding a predicate in the WHERE clause limits the number of rows returned to those that make the predicate TRUE. In the statement below, rows that have DEPTNO = 5 will make the WHERE clause TRUE, so they will be the only rows returned. In our example, there are no employees in department 5, so none will be returned.

    SELECT ENAME
    FROM EMP
    WHERE DEPTNO = 5;

This query has just one condition in the WHERE clause. These operators can be used in conditions in the WHERE clause. For these examples, x=1 and y=2:

Operator	Function	Example
=	Equal	x=1 is TRUE
!=, <>	Not equal	x!=y is TRUE
>	Greater than	y>x is TRUE
<	Less than	x<y is TRUE
>=	Greater than or equal to	x+y >= 2 is TRUE
<=	Less than or equal to	x+2 <= y*2 is TRUE
!<	Not less than	2*x !< y is TRUE
!>	Not greater than	x !> 1 is TRUE
BETWEEN	Between	x BETWEEN 0 AND 5 is TRUE

Each condition is a statement whose truth can be evaluated. The truth value of a condition can be TRUE, FALSE or UNKNOWN. An UNKNOWN truth value can result when null values are present; this situation is discussed on page 38. Here only the truth values TRUE and FALSE are considered.

Combining conditions
Conditions have truth values as their result, and the logical operators AND, OR and NOT are used to combine them. The figure below shows how a predicate would be evaluated for the EMP table row for Smith, who is assigned to department 3 and has salary 150.

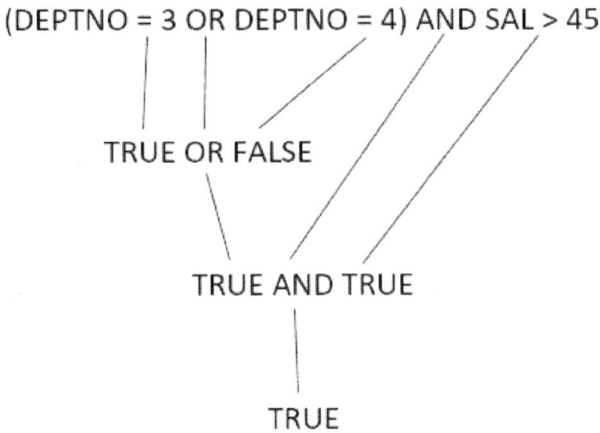

(DEPTNO = 3 OR DEPTNO = 4) AND SAL > 45

TRUE OR FALSE

TRUE AND TRUE

TRUE

Figure 5. Evaluation of a WHERE clause

Missing Values

With earlier database systems, if a file could have some missing values, the application programmer would include logic in the program to deal with that situation, using a sentinel value. The sentinel value, chosen to be outside the possible range of values for that data, would stand for a missing value. If there was no value when data was entered, the application would insert the sentinel value. Upon retrieval, the application would not present it, showing instead a missing value. Of course, the application would have to include logic to exclude the sentinel value from computations made using that column.

After the passage of time, and the evolution of values that may occur in a column, the range of values could grow to include the sentinel value. Then, when the sentinel value appeared, that value would seem to simply disappear! Such problems can be very disruptive and hard to diagnose and resolve.

The designers of SQL changed this situation by introducing null values, that are used to indicate missing values. All the logic and computations of SQL allow for the possibility of null values.

Because the value of a null is unknown, SQL must use three-valued logic to evaluate WHERE clauses. A statement (such as SAL > 100) can be true, false or unknown.

Any comparison with a null value gives the truth value UNKNOWN. That is, comparing some value with an unknown value cannot be either true or false, because you don't know the missing value. Usually, conditions would be combined using two – valued logic. Two-valued logic has the familiar truth tables shown below:

p	q	p or q
F	F	F
F	T	T
T	F	T
T	T	T

p	q	p or q
F	F	F
F	T	T
T	F	T
T	T	T

p	not p
F	T
T	F

Figure 6. Two-Value Truth Tables

Because the example of Figure 5 does not involve any NULL values, it was evaluated using two-valued truth tables.

These are the three-value truth tables used in SQL:

p	q	p and q
F	F	F
F	T	F
T	F	F
T	T	T
F	?	F
T	?	?
?	?	?

p	q	p or q
F	F	F
F	T	T
T	F	T
T	T	T
F	?	?
T	?	T
?	?	?

p	not p
F	T
T	F

Figure 7. Three-Value Truth Tables

Three-value truth tables are a straightforward extension of two-value truth tables. Consider the truth table for AND, for the case F and unknown. We know that for the AND operator, if either operand is false, then AND is false. Thus, if one operand is false, whatever the value of the other operand, the result must be false. For OR, if either operand is true the result is true, so T OR unknown must be true.

Arithmetic with nulls always produces null values. If we add an unknown value to a known value, of course the result can't be known, so it must be null. Consider this example, that uses SQLPLUS to make a table of total compensation.

```
SELECT ENAME, SAL, COMM, SAL + COMM
"TOTAL COMP"
FROM EMP;
```

ENAME	SAL	COMM	TOTAL COMP
SMITH	150		
CHEN	120		
LIU	100		
JONES	20	50	70

The TOTAL COMP column does not show the correct result for most employees because the null value for commission causes the total compensation value to be null. The designers of SQL have solved this problem with the function NVL, that treats a null value as any arithmetic value for a computation.

This statement uses nvl(comm,0) to treat null values of comm as zero.

```
SELECT   ENAM,  SAL,  COMM,  SAL  +
NVL(COMM,0) "TOTAL COMP" FROM EMP:
```

ENAME	SAL	COMM	TOTAL
COMP			
SMITH	150		150
CHEN	120		120
LIU	100		100
JONES	20	50	70

The final aspect of null values is searching for null values. Because the truth value of any comparison with a null value is unknown, how can null values be found? Any comparison with a null will result in an unknown truth value, which will not make the WHERE clause evaluate as true, so the row with the null will never be found.

SQL has special operators to compare to null, IS NULL and IS NOT NULL. For example, the statement

```
SELECT ENAME
FROM EMP
WHERE COMM IS NOT NULL;
```

will list the name of the single employee who earns a commission. An IS NULL comparison evaluates true when the value is null, and false otherwise. Similarly, IS NOT NULL evaluates true when the value is not null, and false if the value is null.

```
SQL> SELECT ENAME
FROM EMP
WHERE COMM IS NULL;
```

ENAME

SMITH

CHEN

LIU

As you've seen, null values introduce some complexity into SQL. However, this complexity allows application programmers to deal with missing values in a systematic way without introducing additional complexity into applications.

String Comparisons

Commonly, a search for a string will involve a partial match, such as a name search if there is uncertainty about how the name is spelled. It might occur for search of some complex identifiers where a match is needed on just part of the identifying number.

SQL includes a string search comparison that can perform a partial match search. The operator is LIKE. When using LIKE for a partial match search, two special characters can be used. The _ character will match any single character, and the % character will match any sequence of zero or more characters.

For example, the comparison X LIKE '%' will match any sequence of zero or more characters, so it will be true for every value of X. These examples show several different comparisons using LIKE on the employee table, and the results produced.

SELECT ENAME
FROM EMP
WHERE ENAME LIKE 'CH%';

ENAME
CHEN

SELECT ENAME
FROM EMP
WHERE ENAME LIKE '%N%';

ENAME
CHEN
JONES

SELECT ENAME
FROM EMP
WHERE ENAME LIKE '%JON_';

ENAME

Membership in a Set

In the WHERE clause, you can also check whether a value is a member of a set. The set can be enumerated in the query by listing it in parentheses:

```
SQL> SELECT ENAME
FROM EMP
WHERE DEPTNO IN (3,5);
```

ENAME

SMITH

CHEN

LIU

JONES

The set can also be the result of a SELECT statement that produces a single-column result:

SELECT ENAME
FROM EMP
WHERE   SAL   >   (SELECT   AVG(SAL)
FROM EMP);

Ordering
This SELECT statement lists the names, employee numbers and salaries in Department 3 in order of employee number

SQL> SELECT ENAME, EMPNO, SAL
FROM EMP
WHERE DEPTNO = 3
ORDER BY EMPNO;

ENAME	EMPNO	SAL
SMITH	20	150
CHEN	30	120

If ORDER BY is followed by DESC, then the results are delivered in descending order:

SELECT ENAME, EMPNO, SAL

FROM EMP
ORDER BY SAL DESC;

ENAME	EMPNO	SAL
SMITH	20	150
CHEN	30	120
LIU	40	100
JONES	50	20

Nesting

You can use a SELECT statement inside another SELECT statement, in the WHERE or HAVING clauses

Data returned by the subquery is used by the outer statement in the same way as a literal value that is present in the WHERE clause:

The subquery is enclosed in parentheses

A subquery that returns more than one row can be used only with multiple value operators such as IN or NOT IN

The subquery must return only one column, unless used for row comparison, when it can return multiple columns

The subquery cannot be a set operation: only single queries are allowed

```
SELECT *
FROM CUSTOMERS
WHERE CUST_ID IN
        (SELECT DISTINCT CUST_ID FROM ORDERS
        WHERE ORDER_VALUE > 5000);
```
Also:

```
SELECT ENAME FROM EMP
WHERE DEPTNO IN
            (SELECT DEPTNO FROM DEPT WHERE
            LOC= 'DC');
```

ENAME
SMITH
CHEN

Aggregate Functions

An aggregate function transforms a column of data into a single value, through some specified operation.

Here's an example. In this case, we're looking for the total of all salaries paid to employees who earn more than 100:

```
SELECT SUM(SAL) FROM EMP WHERE SAL >
100;
```

SUM(SAL)
270

EMP

EMPNO	ENAME	DEPTNO	JOB	MGR	SAL	COMM
20	SMITH	3	PRES		150	
30	CHEN	3	VPRES	20	120	
40	LIU	5	SALES MGR	30	100	
50	JONES	5	SALES REP	40	20	50

Smith and Chen have salaries greater than 100, and the sum of their salaries is 270.

Now let's sum the total commissions:

SELECT SUM (COMM) FROM EMP;

SUM(COMM)
50

You might expect the aggregate function SUM to return a null value from summing all the values of commission, since some of the values are null, and the result of adding null to anything is another null.

Clearly, something else is happening! Aggregate functions ignore nulls. Or you can say that aggregate functions operate on only the values that are present. Clearly, 50 is the sum of all commissions that are paid.

Now let's find the average of commissions over all employees. We no longer expect a null value.

SELECT AVG(COMM) FROM EMP;

AVG(COMM)

50

This is a consistent result, provided you understand the definition of the result that is used. The average of all commissions that are paid is 50.

The most popular aggregate functions are AVG, SUM, COUNT, MAX and MIN, although popular database systems have many other aggregate functions as well. These illustrate the operation of aggregate functions, although you'll want to learn about the aggregate functions for the database system you are using in your own work.

SELECT MAX(SAL), MIN(SAL), COUNT(SAL),
DISTINCT COUNT(SAL)
FROM EMP;

MAX(SAL)	MIN(SAL)	COUNT(SAL)	DISTINCT COUNT(SAL)
150	20	4	4

Arithmetic in the SELECT Clause

The other method for doing computation in a SELECT statement is to perform arithmetic operations in the SELECT clause. Arithmetic operators can be used between column names in the SELECT list, and between column names and constants.

This query shows a list of salaries and what the new salaries would be if each employee is given a 10% raise:

```
SELECT ENAME, SAL, SAL * 1.1 "NEW SAL"
FROM EMP;
```

ENAME	SAL	NEW SAL
SMITH	150	165
CHEN	120	132
LIU	100	110
JONES	20	22

A feature of Oracle SQLPLUS has been used to create the heading "NEW SAL" for the column with the increased salary.

This SELECT statement produces a more complete analysis that includes commission in the computation of compensation, before and after the raise that's being considered:

```
SELECT ENAME "Ename", SAL "Sal", SAL +
NVL(COMM,0) "Comp", SAL* 1.1 "New Sal",
SAL * 1.1 + NVL(COMM,0) " New    Comp"
FROM EMP;
```

Ename	Sal	Comp	New Sal	New Comp
SMITH	150	150	165	165
CHEN	120	120	132	132
LIU	100	100	110	110
JONES	20	70	22	72

Partitioning Into Groups

The result of a SELECT statement can be partitioned into groups by the GROUP BY clause, based on the value of an attribute. Then an aggregate function can be applied on a group-by-group basis. This SELECT statement calculates the average salary by department:

```
SELECT DEPTNO, AVG(SAL)
FROM EMP
GROUP BY DEPTNO;
```

DEPTNO	AVG(SAL)
5	60
3	135

Along with GROUP BY, the HAVING clause can be used to include and exclude groups based on the value of an aggregate function:

```
SELECT DEPTNO, AVG(SAL)
FROM EMP
GROUP BY DEPTNO
HAVING AVG(SAL) > 100;
```

DEPTNO	AVG(SAL)
3	135

A SELECT statement can include both a HAVING clause and a WHERE clause; they do not contradict or interfere with each other. The WHERE clause determines which rows are retrieved by the SELECT statement. Those rows are then used to form groups as directed by the GROUP BY clause. Finally, the HAVING statement determines which groups are produced as output and are evaluated by aggregate functions in the SELECT list.

```
SELECT DEPTNO
FROM EMP
WHERE JOB LIKE 'SALES%'
GROUP BY DEPTNO
HAVING COUNT(*) >= 2;
```

DEPTNO
5

Selecting from Multiple Tables
Clearly, it's essential that a SELECT statement be able to relate information in one table to information that's in another table. There are two ways to accomplish this:

1. Set operations can be performed to combine the results of several SELECT statements, provided that the results of the statements have compatible definitions.

2. A join can be used. A join is a SELECT statement that uses values stored in two tables to relate them to each other, retrieving data from those tables.

Recall that using SQL, we don't tell the database system how to process the query; instead, the desired result is defined using SQL, then the database system decides how to process it. In the early days of relational database, there was a widely held view that no relational database system could ever provide adequate performance, because there are no physical pointers between tables to make joins work faster.

Two developments have improved the performance of relational systems so that today they far exceed these expectations:

1. Fantastic improvements in overall computer performance, and
2. Improvements in algorithms (discussed in Chapter 8).

The IBM 3081, a typical mainframe of 1980, with a typical installation filling a large room, cost $3.7 million, with a compute speed of about 3.5 million instructions per second, or MIPS. By 2018, an Intel i9-9900K chip, that would be incorporated into a $2,000 personal computer, cost about $350, offering more than 400,000 MIPS.[11]   Thus, computing power increased by more than a factor of 100,000 and the cost decreased by a factor of *about 2,000 for a combined gain of MIS per dollar of 200 million!*

The use of cost-based optimization for access path selection produced gains in query processing statements that can also be as large as a factor of

---

[11]   Wikipedia, *Instructions per second,* *https://en.wikipedia.org/wiki/Instructions_per_second,* *accessed August 2021.*

1,000,000 in some cases, compared with earlier methods.

Set Operations

Although SQL is a bag language, these operations are traditional set operations, producing results that are sets. Thus, duplicates are automatically eliminated. For example, If the same result is produced twice as the result of UNION, it will have just one occurrence in the result.

These familiar operators from set theory are used in SQL to combine the results of SELECT statements:

INTERSECT—elements appearing in both results

UNION—elements appearing in either result

MINUS—elements in the first result that are not in the second result

For example:

```
SELECT DEPTNO
FROM DEPT
MINUS
SELECT DEPTNO FROM EMP;


DEPTNO
   1
   2
```

Join

This query is called a *join* because a mental picture of the join is that each row of the first table is pasted to each row of the second table; then the WHERE clause is applied row by row to the pasted-together row.

The example below is called an *equi-join* because the rows are connected based on equal values of a column in each table, namely the DEPTNO column.

> SELECT ENAME, LOC
>
> FROM   EMP,   DEPT
> WHERE   EMP.DEPTNO=DEPT.DEPTNO;

ENAME		LOC
SMITH		DC
CHEN	DC	
LIU	LA	
JONES		LA

Conceptually, the join pastes together rows of the two tables, creating a pasted row with a row from each table every time the join criterion is met. In this case, whenever the DEPT.DEPTNO matches EMP.DEPTNO, a row is produced that's a combination of the two rows. Think of pasting every row of EMP onto every row of DEPT—which would make a "pasted" table of 12 rows—and then applying the join criterion to eliminate all those that didn't have matching values of department number.

Although this is good way to understand the result of a join query, it's not the way joins are processed, because this method would be inefficient. Chapter 8 describes how joins are processed, and the role you can play in improving the performance of joins in your own programs.

Performance of join operations is the most important aspect of performance of relational database systems—and of your programs that use database systems. A join query can involve many tables, although a join is always processed two tables at a time. Join processing is discussed in Chapter 8.

Self-Join
To discover relationships between rows within a table, the table can be joined to itself. Suppose we are looking for employees who earn more than their supervisors:

```
SELECT EMP, EMP MGR
FROM EMP, EMP MGR
WHERE EMP.MGR = MGR.EMPNO
AND EMP.SAL > MGR.SAL;
```

In the select list, EMP appears twice. The second time, it is followed by MGR, an *alias* for EMP. The alias allows the query to be written like a join involving an EMP table and an MGR table.

All the employees in the EMP table earn less than their supervisors, so this query won't retrieve any results. One row can be changed so that there will be a result, using the UPDATE statement:

```
UPDATE EMP
SET SAL = 160
WHERE EMPNO = 30;


1 row updated
```

Now the same query will produce a result, since CHEN now earns more than her manager:

ENAME
CHEN

Outer Join

To explore outer join, a new example is needed. Consider these tables of customers and orders, and suppose we want to produce a list of all customers and orders. What happens to the result of the join when a customer hasn't placed an order, or we have an order placed by a customer not in CUSTOMERS? A customer without an order or an order without a customer would not appear in the result.

CUSTOMERS

CUST_ID	CNAME	LOC
25	ACME	NYC
36	KOJO	DEN
48	BOXER	DC
22	JADA	ATL
16	GLAD	DC

ORDERS

ORDER_ID	CUST_ID	ORDER_DATE	TOTAL
56	36	6/11/2015	591
57	36	7/14/2015	5147
58	48	9/18/2016	269
59	22	12/13/2016	48526
60	36	5/22/2017	23
61	2	5/13/2018	6574
62	16	7/19/2019	624

There are five customers, and over time, seven orders have been placed. One of the customers, ACME, has not placed any orders. In addition, the ORDERS table shows that an order has been placed by customer number 2, who does not appear in the CUSTOMER table. This figure shows how ACME and order 61 would be missed by an inner join:

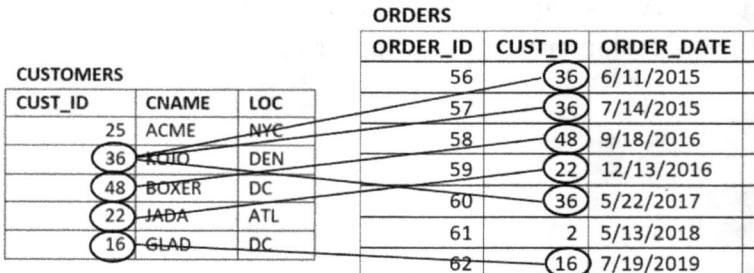

Figure 8. Rows missed by inner join query

Note as well that a report of the total value of orders placed by customer would have problems:

```
SELECT CNAME, SUM(TOTAL)
FROM CUSTOMERS, ORDERS
WHERE          CUSTOMERS.CUST#     =
ORDERS.CUST#
GROUP BY CNAME;
```

CNAME	SUM(TOTAL)
BOXER	269
JADA	48526
KOJO	5761
GLAD	624

ACME is a customer who has placed a total of 0 in orders; ACME Is not shown on the report, because there was no row in ORDERS for ACME's customer number. Similarly, the order placed by customer 2 does not appear anywhere in the report, because there is no customer with customer number 2 in CUSTOMERS.

The outer join gives us a way to deal with these non-matching rows.

Right Outer Join
The right outer join produces all the results of an inner join, plus the rows of the right-hand table that

would not be retrieved by the inner join. In this case, that would be the order from customer 2:

SELECT   CNAME,   ORDER_ID, ORDER_DATE, TOTAL
FROM CUSTOMERS
RIGHT OUTER JOIN ORDERS
ON   CUSTOMERS.CUST_ID   = ORDERS.CUST_ID;

CNAME	ORDER_ID	ORDER_DAT
TOTAL		
KOJO	56	11-JUN-15
591		
KOJO	57	14-JUL-15
5147		
BOXER	58	18-SEP-16
269		
JADA	59	13-DEC-16
48526		
KOJO	60	22-MAY-17
23		
	61	13-MAY-18
6574		
GLAD	62	19-JUL-19
624		

Left Outer Join
The left outer join is the counterpart of the right outer join; it returns all the results of the inner join, plus

the rows from the left-hand table that would not be retrieved by the inner join. In this case, that would be

```
SELECT CNAME, ORDER_ID, ORDER_DATE,
TOTAL
FROM CUSTOMER
LEFT OUTER JOIN ORDERS ON
CUSTOMERS.CUST_D – ORDERS.CUST_ID;
```

CNAME	ORDER ID	ORDER DAT
TOTAL		
KOJO	56	11-JUN-15
591		
KOJO	57	14-JUL-15
5147		
BOXER	58	18-SEP-16
269		
JADA	59	13-DEC-16
48526		
KOJO	60	22-MAY-17
23		
GLAD	62	19-JUL-19
624		
ACME		

7 rows selected.

The left inner join retrieved ACME's name, although ACME has no entries in ORDERS.

Non-Equi Join

All the joins considered have been based on equality of values between two tables, so they are all called equi-joins. It is also possible for a join to be based on an inequality. Like outer joins, non equi-joins are not used frequently. One use is to categorize values into categories based on ranges.

As an example, suppose a company had salary ranges, and categorized an employee's salary based on those ranges:

SALGRADE

GRADE#	LOWSAL	HIGHSAL
1	20	50
2	50	75
3	75	100
4	100	125
5	125	150
6	150	175

Figure 9. Salary Ranges

To list the salary grades for employees, the non equi-join query would be

```
SELECT ENAME, GRADE#
FROM EMP, SALGRADE
WHERE SAL BETWEEN LOWSAL AND
HIGHSAL;
```

2.8   Data Manipulation
SQL uses three statements to change values stored in the database:

INSERT adds new rows to the database

DELETE removes rows from the database

UPDATE changes specific values in one or more rows

There are two forms of the INSERT statement. The most general is:

    INSERT INTO TABLE_NAME (column list)
    VALUES (value list);

where column list is the list of columns that are to receive values, and value list is the list of values to be inserted. You do not have to list all the columns in the table, and you do not have to insert values into all the columns. Of course, you must list at least all columns that have the NO NULL constraint.

The second form can be used when you are inserting values into every column:

    INSERT INTO TABLE_NAME VALUES (value list);

Here is an example of the first form, using a column list:

    INSERT INTO EMP
    (EMPNO, ENAME, JOB, SAL, COMM,

```
DEPTNO)
VALUES
(20,'CHEN','PRES',150, NULL, 3);
```

The general form of the DELETE statement is:

```
DELETE
FROM table_name
WHERE predicate;
```

An example of a simple DELETE statement, deleting everyone who earns more than 100, is

```
DELETE
FROM EMP
WHERE SAL >= 100;
```

A SELECT statement can be nested in the WHERE clause, like this:

```
DELETE
FROM EMP
WHERE SAL >
        (SELECT AVG(SAL) FROM EMP);
```

The general form of the UPDATE statement is

```
UPDATE table_name
SET
        column1= value1,
        column1=value2,
```

```
column3=value3,
....
WHERE  predicate;
```

A simple update of a single row is

```
UPDATE EMP
SET JOB = 'SALES MGR'
WHERE EMPNO = 'JONES';
```

Like INSERT, In the UPDATE statement, values in another table can be used to control the UPDATE, like this:

```
UPDATE EMP
SET SAL = SAL * 1.1
WHERE EMPNO IN
        (SELECT AVG(SAL) FROM EMP);
```

2.9   Data Definition

The data definition statements in SQL allow you to create, alter and drop database objects such as tables and indexes.

CREATE creates a new database object
ALTER changes an existing database object
DROP removes an existing database object

CREATE, ALTER TABLE

The general form of the CREATE TABLE statement is

```
CREATE TABLE table_name(
column1 datatype,
column2 datatype,
column3 datatype,
...
columnN datatype,
PRIMARY KEY (column_list),
FOREIGN KEY(column_list)   references
(table_name)
);
```

This example creates the familiar EMP table:

```
CREATE TABLE EMP(
EMPNO INTEGER NOT NULL,
ENAME VARCHAR(20) NOT NULL,
DEPTNO INTEGER,
JOB VARCHAR(20) NOT NULL,
SAL INTEGER NOT NULL,
COMM INTEGER,
PRIMARY KEY (EMPNO),
FOREIGN KEY (MGR) REFERENCES
EMP (EMPNO)
);
```

For this table, the business has decided that a new employee can't be added to the database until they have an employee number, their name is known, their job is decided, and the salary has been set, although their department might not yet be decided. These business decisions result in the NOT NULL constraints established in the CREATE TABLE statement.

The contents of the MGR column are required to be an employee number.

The ALTER TABLE statement is used to add and remove columns from a table, change the data type of a table, or change integrity constraints.

To add a column to a table, the form of the statement is

ALTER TABLE table_name ADD COLUMN column_name;

The form to drop a column is
ALTER TABLE table_name DROP COLUMN column_name;

The statement can also be used to change the data type or constraints on a column as follows:
ALTER TABLE table_name MODIFY COLUMN column_name datatype;
ALTER TABLE table_name MODIFY COLUMN Column_name datatype NOT NULL;

For example, this statement could be used to add a social security number to the EMP table:

ALTER TABLE EMP

ADD COLUMN SSN VARCHAR(9) NO NULL
AFTER JOB;

CREATE, ALTER INDEX

The CREATE statement is also used to create
indexes. An index is like a phone directory, where
you use last name to look up a phone number. In this
case, the database system uses a column value to find
the location of a row containing that value.

Indexes speed up queries based on the column (or
columns) that they index, but since they need to be
maintained when values are changed, they slow
down updates and inserts.

The CREATE INDEX statement allows you to name
the index, specify the table and columns that it will
index, and indicate whether the index will be used to
enforce uniqueness of the values that it indexes.

Note that although each index is given a name, that
name is not referenced by SQL statements that might
use the index to access data—the name is used only
by ALTER INDEX and DROP INDEX statements.
The CREATE INDEX statement changes the
physical structure of the database but does not affect
the relational view of data used by the application.

Recall that one of the basic goals of the relational
approach is for the database system to decide how to
process a query, not the programmer. Thus, the

database system makes the decision about whether to use an index, as part of its process to determine its overall method to process each SQL statement. That topic is covered in Chapter 8.

To speed up searches of the employee table by employee name, create an index on the ENAME column with this statement:

> CREATE INDEX EMP_INDEX
> ON EMP (ENAME);

CREATE VIEW
A view is a stored query, with a result that is accessed like a table. A view is commonly used to restrict access to some columns of a table, or to derive complex results that are frequency used, to simplify queries.

Suppose the clerk for department 3 is permitted to view name, employee number and job but not salary data. A view for the clerk's use could be created using this CREATE VIEW statement:

> CREATE VIEW DEPT3 AS
> > SELECT EMPNO, ENAME, JOB FROM
> > EMP
> > WHERE DEPTNO = 3;

Once the clerk is given access to DEPT3, the view can be queried the same way as a table. The clerk will not see the salary information or even be able to find out about the underlying EMP table.

DROP

The DROP statement is used to remove objects from the database. Some examples are:

    DROP TABLE EMP;

    DROP VIEW DEPT3;

    DROP INDEX EMP_INDEX;

2.10   Data Control

The data control features of SQL establish who has access to information stored in the database, and who can carry out which actions on the database.

CREATE USER

Before a user can access a database, the user must be created:

    CREATE USER Jada IDENTIFIED BY password;

The CREATE USER statement creates the user and establishes the password. At this point, though, the user has no privileges.

GRANT, REVOKE

The first privilege is to connect to the database, given with the GRANT statement:

    GRANT CONNECT TO Jada;

Now Jada can connect to the database, but she can't access any data, unless access has already been granted to PUBLIC, which would allow her to access it. This statement allows her to query, add or delete rows in the EMP table, but not update them:

> GRANT SELECT, INSERT, DELETE ON
> EMP TO Jada;

This GRANT statement is a quick way to grant all privileges, including update:

> GRANT ALL ON EMP TO JADA WITH
> GRANT OPTION;

WITH GRANT OPTION allows JADA to grant these privileges to others.

DROP USER

When JADA leaves the project, her accesses can be ended with a DROP USER JADA statement.

ROLES

If a specific job carries with it a lot of database privileges, revoking those privileges from someone who leaves the job and then granting them to the replacement can be an onerous task. That's the purpose of ROLEs in SQL.

A ROLE is created, and a group of privileges is assigned to a ROLE. Then that ROLE can be GRANTed to a user, and later REVOKEd from a user. Those single GRANT and REVOKE statements can assign and remove hundreds of privileges at once.

These are the statements to create a ROLE of Clerk, GRANT privileges to that role, then GRANT the ROLE to Jada.

> CREATE ROLE Clerk IDENTIFIED BY
> "password";

GRANT ALL ON EMP TO Clerk;
GRANT ALL ON DEPT TO Clerk;
GRANT CLERK TO Jada;

When Jada leaves the department, and is replaced by Kendall, then the transfer of privileges is accomplished with two SQL statements:

REVOKE Clerk FROM Jada;
GRANT Clerk TO Kendall;

If Kendall is to have fewer privileges than Jada, then some of Jada's previous privileges can be REVOKED from Kendall:

REVOKE ALL ON DEPT FROM Kendall;

Chapter 3   Normalization, Denormalization

3.1   Introduction

Normalization is a collection of principles developed to define what is a "good" relational data model. Usually, normalization is presented from a theoretical point of view, making it hard to apply these valuable ideas to a real problem. Here a different approach is taken. We start with a set of rules in plain English – Roberts's Rules -- that result in a highly normalized database. Then we discuss normalization theory. Finally, we explore the relationship between the rules and each normal form.

The goal of this chapter is to provide a working understanding of both Roberts's Rules and the principles of normalization, so that you can apply normalization to your own data models, and so that you can explain normalization to your peers without resorting to a lot of theory.

Normalization is important. Designing the structure of a database, called the *data model*, decides the names of the tables and the columns that each includes. When programs are written, those table names and their contents are coded into application programs; if the data model changes after programs have been written, extensive, costly changes may be needed. If there are hundreds of programs accessing the database, such changes can cripple a programming project.

The goal is to develop a *robust* data model, that won't require change during the project, or even afterward, to minimize such disruptive programming changes. Normalization gives us criteria that we can apply to a data model to judge its robustness.

Syntax and Semantics
Normalization is said to be a *semantic* concept because it deals with the underlying meaning of data, not just the values that are present. That meaning is taken from the real-world problem that is being addressed and includes all the rules that apply to the data, such as limitations on permitted values.

Data can be divided into two classes: *extensional* and *intentional*. Extensional data is the data values that are present in the database. It is a subset of the intentional data, which is all the data values that are permitted to be in the database. Intentional data is determined by the constraints on the data that are imposed by real-world conditions; thus, normalization is concerned with intentional data.

Examples of such constraints from our example of the EMP table could be an upper limit on salary, or a requirement that the MGR attribute value be a valid employee number, or a requirement that the DEPTNO attribute value be a valid identifier of a department from the DEPT table.

All the different normal forms -- and Roberts's Rules -- are semantic notions. Therefore, you can't simply look at what data is present and decide whether a given table of a relational database is in some form or not. You must understand not just what's present, but also what are the permissible values for data in the table.

3.2   Entities and Entity Types
An entity is something in the world outside the computer that we record information about in the database. An *entity type* is a set of similar things that we store information about. An *entity instance* is one example of some entity type. For example, *employee* is an entity type--it's a set of all employees of a company. And a single employee is an entity instance, an example of the entity type employee.

Much of our discussion of normalization deals with identifying entity types and their attributes.   In a single relational table, we capture information about a single entity type; and each row of that table contains information about an entity instance. The choice of the entity types in the real world that are modeled in the database, and their associated attributes, makes up the data model, the structure of the relational database.   If the right data model is chosen, it can be stable while many changes are made to the programs that use it over the years.

3.3   Relations

A relational database is a set of tables, formally called relations. Since a relation looks like a table and is accessed like a table, the term *table* is used throughout this book. The purpose of a relational database is to model in information some circumstance in the real world. A table is used for each entity type; and within each table, each row corresponds to a single instance of that entity.

Facts

The framework used here to understand normalization is based on Bill Kent's *Fact-Based Data Analysis*[12]. Each row is an ordered collection of *facts* about a single instance of an entity--the value of each attribute conveys one fact about the entity instance described by that row. For example, the table below corresponds to the entity type *employees* and each row corresponds to a single employee, an instance of that entity type. In each row, each attribute of each row is a single fact about that instance of an employee.

EMPNO	ENAME	JOB	DEPTNO
10	Wu	President	1
20	Liu	VP	2
30	Chen	VP	2

---

[12] Kent, William. Fact-based analysis and design. *The Journal of Systems and Software* 4 (1984), 99-121.

A fact has two parts: a subject that is characterized by the fact, and a value. For a fact to be duplicated, both the subject and the value must be identical.

In the employee table, even though the value 2 for DEPTNO appears more than once, this is not the duplication of a fact. In the row for Liu, the value 2 for DEPTNO indicates that Liu is assigned to department 2; in the row for Chen, the value 2 for DEPTNO indicates that Chen is assigned to department 2. These are two different facts. The appearance of the same value for an attribute in two different rows may not be the repetition of a fact.

At this point, we are concerned only with *single-valued* facts, such as the fact that Wu is assigned to Department 2. If the operating procedures of the organization permit Wu to be assigned to just one department, then we say that this is a single-valued fact. Later on, in the discussion of Fourth Normal Form, the notion of fact will be extended to include multi-valued facts, that can have multiple values simultaneously. If the organization allowed an employee to be assigned to two departments at once, for example, then this fact would be multi-valued.

3.4   Data Modeling

A relational database is a set of relations; it is a *model* of something in the real world, so the overall design of a database is called a *data model.* The formality of normalization gives us criteria for designing data models that help to avoid problems we might otherwise discover later as code is being written. Data modeling is the subject of Chapter 4.

3.5 What Comes Next

In the discussion that follows, Roberts's Rules are presented first, a collection of rules in plain English about how to design a database. These rules are based on the permitted content of the database and provide a commonsense way to construct a data model, without any use of theory.

The application of all four of Roberts's Rules will result in a database that is fully normalized, but also has additional strengths that go beyond just the issues that are dealt with in normalization theory.

We carefully explore Roberts's Rules, to get practical criteria to design a high-quality data model. Roberts's Rules can also be a way to teach others about normalization, using a framework that doesn't involve abstract theory.

Following Roberts's Rules, we cover the most important normal forms: first normal form, second normal form, third normal form, Boyce-Codd normal form, and fourth normal form. For each, just enough theory to define and understand it is included. Finally, the consequences of each are covered: how does each normal form improve the quality of the data model?

Finally, we look at the correspondence of the normal forms with Roberts's Rules.

3.6   Roberts's Rules

Roberts's Rule One

Roberts's Rule One: each table describes exactly one entity type.

Each table models a single entity type, and each row of the table models one instance of that entity type. Rule One disallows facts about two different entity types in one table, which also precludes putting facts about one entity type in two different tables.

The modified version of the employee table shown below has added department name in addition to just department number. With the previous version of the table, we already knew that, for example, Wu was assigned to department 1. Telling us that department 1 is the headquarters department doesn't tell us anything more about Wu. The department name is a fact about the department and not a fact about the employee. This example violates Rule One.

EMPNO	ENAME	JOB	DEPTNO	DNAME
10	Wu	President	1	HQ
20	Liu	VP	2	Sales
30	Chen	VP	2	Sales

Roberts's Rule Two

Roberts's Rule Two: each fact is represented only once in the database.

It's important that each fact be stored only once in the database. You might think that this is to save space; however, with the cost of disk storage, except for the largest databases, the cost of duplicating a fact is small.

Rule Two's important benefit is that it improves data integrity. If a single fact is represented more than once in the database, that fact must be changed in two—or three or four—places every time its value changes. The programmers who write the application know where all the values are and () will update all of them when they change. However, over time, people change jobs, so new programmers take over maintenance who may not know about all the copies of each fact. This problem can cause applications to behave in a bizarre fashion.

Consider the example portrayed by the figure below. Note that the same values for DEPTNO appear in both tables. Is this a violation of Rule Two?

EMPNO	ENAME	JOB	SAL	DEPTNO
34	Liu	Pres	200	5
456	Chen	VP	150	5
32	Cox	Sales	75	9

DEPTNO	DNAME	LOC
5	HQ	NYC
9	Sales	DC
20	Research	SF

Figure 10. Rule 2 Illustration

The example in Figure 10 does not violate Rule Two, even though the same values appear with the same column names. Rule Two states that the same *fact* must not be represented more than once. A fact has a value and a subject. The values for DEPTNO in EMP each portray the fact of an employee's assignment to a particular department, so each is a fact about the employee entity type. The values for DEPTNO in DEPT each portray the department number of a given department; each is a fact about a department. Thus, the same facts are not represented more than once.

Roberts's Rule Three

Roberts's Rule Three: each row can be stored in only one table.

This rule, due to Chris Date[13], prohibits one specific type of data model. That's the use of tables as stages along a production line. For example, suppose a multi-table data model is used for the process of recruiting a new employee. The first table might be applicants, the second might be those awaiting reference checks, the third might be those who had their physicals, and the fourth might be those who are ready to start work. Using this concept, an applicant's row would move from one table to another to show progression through the recruiting and hiring process.

This approach has several problems:

---

[13] Date, C.J. Column in *Datamation*, c. 1980.

An application searching for the status of an employee will have to look in four or five different tables to find that person. The SQL data language does not make this convenient or efficient.

A row that moves from table to table must be deleted from the first table and then inserted into the second table. Inserts and deletes are costly operations in terms of computing resources.

More important, this approach incorporates aspects of the business process into the data model. The business process has four stages, so the data model has four tables. What if, tomorrow, the business decides to add a fifth stage in the process between two other stages? Now a new table must be added to the data model and programs must move rows around differently, potentially causing far-reaching code changes in the applications that access this data.

On the other hand, applicant status can be represented by a single attribute, with the rows for all applicants in a single table. In this case, if a new stage is added to the business process the only change is adding one more value for status, a simple change to an application and no change to the data model.

Instead of using tables as models of production line stations, it's easy to track the status of something going through a process with a single status attribute in each row. Then a candidate's row stays in the same table throughout the processing cycle.

Roberts's Rules   91

Roberts's Rule Four

Roberts's Rule Four: If the cardinality of an attribute is greater than one, then the database model must be insensitive to cardinality of that attribute.

It's easy to presume that the cardinality of attributes and collections of attributes will remain the same over time. It's also easy to make assumptions about what a maximum cardinality can be for some attribute. As an example, consider a group of attributes about education. How many college degrees might one employee have earned? I always thought that three would be enough, until I met someone who had five. He broke personnel systems that assumed no one would have more than three degrees.

A good example of a multivalued attribute is telephone number. Once, each of us had a single personal telephone number, that rang in a wired landline at home. Today we might have a landline at home, and we might have a mobile phone. We might have a phone number at work. We might even have a work mobile phone. This assumption of single-valuedness that was once valid is no longer valid.

An organization using a database that allows for only a single value for a telephone number doesn't have a straightforward way to store and retrieve all an employee's telephone numbers. In an emergency, the organization could fail to contact the employee because of a missing telephone number.

There can also be multiple values for home addresses. Some people have vacation homes. There could be multiple business addresses if someone has more than one job. There can be multiple email addresses; each of us has several email addresses.

What's the approach to take if a single attribute or a group of attributes might be multivalued? We make that attribute or group of attributes its own entity type; that is, we put it in a separate table. We identify each row with the identification of its parent entity. Such an entity type is called a *dependent* entity, since it has meaning in the database only if it has a *parent* entity type.

For example, for telephone number, we might create a separate table of telephone numbers, with each row identified by, perhaps, the social security number of the corresponding employee. This table would have one row for each different telephone number of each employee. If one employee had 10 telephone numbers that's fine--we could represent that situation.

Equivalence of Rule One and Rule Two

An interesting question is whether Rule One and Rule Two are equivalent. They can be said to be equivalent if they define the same set of relations. That is, if every relation that satisfies Rule One also satisfies Rule Two and if every relation that satisfies Rule Two also satisfies Rule One then they are equivalent.

Upon first inspection, it appears that Rule One and Rule Two are equivalent. For example, in the expansion of the employee table on page 87, when the department name was added in addition to department number, we said that table violated Rule One because it added a fact about the department entity type into the employee table. But consider department 2 in that table, with two employees assigned to it. The fact that department 2 is the Sales department now appears twice in the employee table, so this table violates Rule Two in addition. Whether Rule One and Rule Two are equivalent is left as an exercise.

The decision about which attributes may be or may become multi-valued is a judgment call to be made, based on the use of the data and the organization's processes and operation. When there is doubt about whether an attribute can be multi-valued, it is best to represent it as multi-valued, because the cost of storing a single-valued fact is small compared with the problems that occur when the database models a multi-valued fact as single-valued.

3.7   Normalization

Normalization theory was developed to provide a framework for guiding the design of relational databases so that a data model could be developed that would be robust and would not need to be changed as the programs accessing the data model evolved and changed over the years. There are normal forms other than the five that are described here; however, several authors of leading books on data modeling, who are themselves data modeling consultants, have told me that in the course of their careers they have not needed any normal forms other than the ones in this book.

The description of a normal form generally follows an established pattern. First, a type of database behavior that's undesirable, called an anomaly, is described, motivating the need for the new normal form. Then, a definition is given of the new normal form. Finally, it is demonstrated that this new normal form prevents the anomalous behavior.

It is possible to use this decomposition approach to design a relational data model, although there are other approaches. The discussion of data modeling in Chapter 4 provides recommendations in this area.

Anomalies

Anomalies fall into broad classes called insert anomalies, delete anomalies, and update anomalies. An example of an insert anomaly would be if, to enter information about some new entity instance, first we had to enter information about different entity type. An example of a delete anomaly would occur if deleting a row deleted information about more than one entity. An example of an update anomaly would be a requirement that to change the value of a single fact we were required to change many stored values in the database.

Basic Concepts

An *entity type* is a class of object that we record information about, and an entity type is modeled by a table in a relational database. An *attribute* is a characteristic of an entity. Some attributes of an employee might be the job that they do, their salary, the date hired the department they're assigned to and so forth. Attributes are modeled as columns in a table. An *entity instance* is a single occurrence of a member of an entity of some type. An entity instance is modeled by a single row of a table in a relational database.

A *candidate key* is a set of attributes a_i, a_j, ... a_k with two time-invariant properties:

> Uniqueness—no two tuples have the same value for the candidate key

> Minimality—if any a_i is discarded from the candidate key, then the uniqueness property is lost.

That is, a candidate key is a single attribute or a group of attributes that uniquely identifies rows. A key that is made up of more than one attribute is called a *composite key.*

The *primary key* is a candidate key selected to be the primary identifier of rows. Any candidate key can be used as the primary key; the choice is usually made based on the usefulness of the attribute that is the primary key.

Functional Dependence

A functional dependence is a particular relationship between two attributes within a table. Attribute X, typically the primary key, is said to *determine* attribute Y, typically a non-key attribute, if every occurrence of a value of X uniquely determines the value of Y.

If X is the primary key, then X is a unique identifier of rows, as well as the entity instance that is described by the row. For example, EMPNO identifies an employee in our example, as well as a row in the EMP table. It's evident that for every occurrence of a value of EMPNO that appears along with a value of SAL, the value of SAL must be that employee's salary. Thus, we say that EMPNO determines SAL in this example, or that SAL is dependent on EMPNO.

We indicate functional dependence with arrows, as in R.X $\rightarrow$ R.Y, read "R.X *determines* R.Y", that is, the X attribute of table R determines the Y attribute of table R. Formally, given relation R, attribute Y of R is *functionally dependent* on attribute X of R if and only if each X-value in R has associated with it precisely one Y-value in R (at any one time).

The diagram below shows an example table with two columns X and Y.

For the values shown, X determines Y. Observe that every time X has value 1 the corresponding value for Y is A. For X = 2, Y always has value C. For X = 3, Y always has value B. X = 4 and X = 6 have only one occurrence, so they always have a single value of Y associated with that value of X. Therefore, we can say that X determines Y.

But Y does not determine X. For value A of Y we have the value 1 and the value 4 for X. Therefore, Y does not determine X in the example and, more broadly, if X determines Y it is not necessarily true that Y determines X.

X	Y
1	A
2	C
3	B
1	A
2	C
4	A
3	B
6	B

In general, determinants are identifiers. A determinant identifies an entity instance, and the attributes that it determines describe that instance.

Full Functional Dependence
Let X and Y be two different attributes of some table R. They may each be a single attribute or be made up of multiple attributes, *simple* or *composite,* respectively. We say that Y is *fully functionally dependent* on X if and only if X determines Y and no

subset of X determines Y. That is, X is the smallest collection of columns that determines Y.

An example of a composite key could be the combination of name and mobile telephone number to identify people. Of course, more than one person can have the same name, and more than one person can share a telephone. But how often will two people with the same name share the same telephone? Thus, name and mobile telephone number makes an appealing composite key.

Using the terminology of Roberts's Rules (coming soon), we would say that the notion of functional dependency deals with "aboutness". The determining attribute identifies the instance, and the determined attribute is a value "about" the instance.

Functional Dependency Diagrams
Functional dependency diagrams (FDDs) illustrate the functional dependencies in a table. There are no standards for these diagrams, so other authors construct FDDs differently. However, the approach used here appears to be the most popular, and is easy to understand, and the se diagrams can be drawn easily with simple drawing tools.

Each FDD shows all the functional dependencies for one table. Each attribute shown as a rectangle, and functional dependencies are shown as arrows from the determinant to the determined.

For example, the EMP table has this FDD:

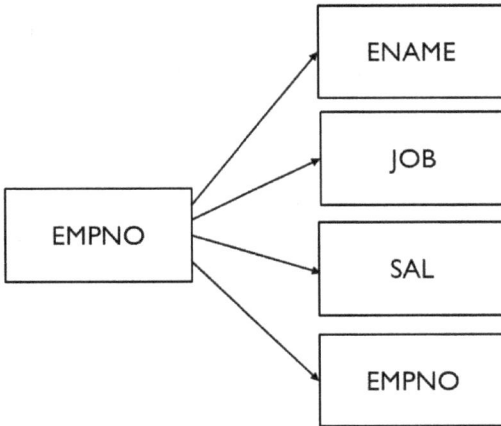

Figure 11. FDD for EMP

A composite determinant, comprised of two or more attributes, is shown with nesting rectangles. This example is for a table of suppliers and parts, where the company can purchase the same part from different suppliers, and separately tracks the inventory of parts from each supplier:

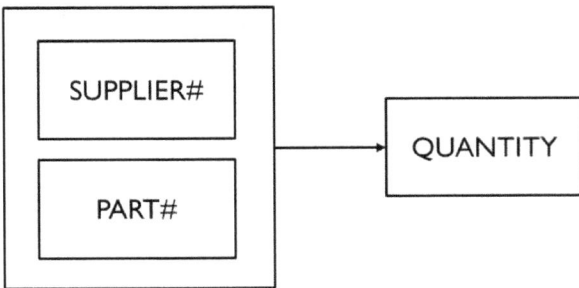

Figure 12. Composite Key Example FDD

There can be transitive dependencies, where one attribute determines a second attribute, that in turn determines a third attribute. In these cases, it is also true that the first attribute determines the third; however, these transitive dependencies are omitted from functional dependency diagrams.

Consider the FDD below, describing a table with a STATUS for SUPPLIER that is an attribute of the CITY where the supplier is located. Thus, STATUS is determined by CITY:

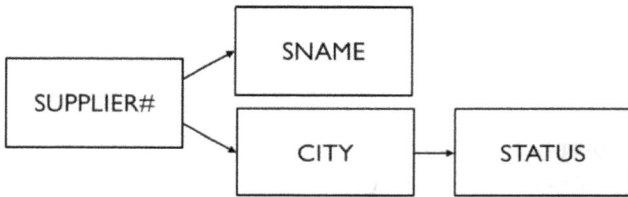

Figure 13. Transitive Dependency FDD

Here, because CITY → STATUS and SUPPLIER# → CITY, it must be the case that each value of SUPPLIER# must be associated with only one value of STATUS, so SUPPLIER# → STATUS. Whenever there is a chain of dependencies like this, by definition there is also this second dependency. By convention, transitive dependencies are not portrayed on FDDs.

Every attribute is shown on a table's FDD, even if it doesn't participate in any relationships. For example, if the attribute sky color was added to the EMP table, where the color of the sky isn't determined by any of the other attributes in the table, this would be its FDD:

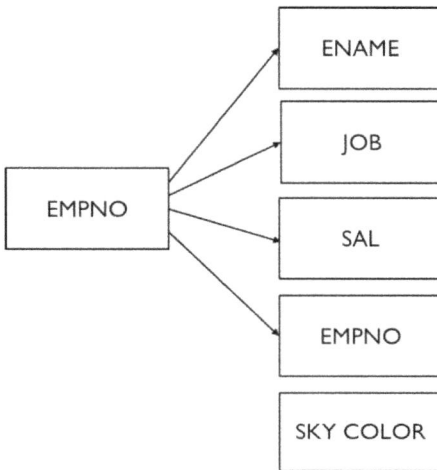

Figure 14. FDD with Undetermined Attribute

3.8 Normal Forms

Normalization theory gives us many normal forms; five of them that are encountered often are included here. These normal forms constitute the language that's used to discuss these concepts, so it's important to understand them.

First Normal Form

A relation is said to be in first normal form if every attribute of every row is atomic.

Ted Codd himself, originator of the relational approach, formulated First Normal Form.14 The word "atomic" is used here in the original Greek sense: that is, it cannot be subdivided (the ancient Greeks didn't know that atoms could be subdivided).

---

[14] Codd, Edgar F. Further normalization of the database relational model. *ACM Transactions on Database Systems* 4 (Dec. 1979), 397-434.

Applied to attributes, it means that an attribute must be a single value. It can't be a list; it can't be another relation.

EMP

EMPNO	ENAME	JOB	EDUCATION	DEPTNO
33	JONES	PRES	BS EE, MS EE, PHD COMP SCI	3
324	CHU	VP	BS EE, MBA	3
88	KUMAR	SALES	BS EE, MA COMM	4
65	YU	QUALITY CONTROL	BS CS, MS CS, PHD CS	5

This example shows an employee table that's not in First Normal Form. The education column has, for each row, a list of degrees that are held, rather than a single value. When an attribute can have several different values, it is called multi-valued, or a repeating value, or if a group of attributes can have several values, a repeating group. Such values cannot be represented as single attributes in a table.

This table exhibits anomalous behavior. If Chu receives a new degree, then to enter that information into the database, our program must

- retrieve a list of Chu's degrees from the database,
- parse the list to find the right place to insert the new degree,
- insert the new degree in the proper place, and finally
- execute an update statement to store the new value for the list in the table.

To convert this information into First Normal Form, the lists are removed from the EMP table and placed into a separate table, like this:

EMP

EMPNO	ENAME	JOB	DEPTNO
33	JONES	PRES	3
324	CHU	VP	3
88	KUMAR	SALES	4
65	YU	QUALITY CONTROL	5

EDUCATION

EMPNO	DEGREE
33	BS EE
33	MS EE
33	PHD COMP SCI
324	BS EE
324	MBA
88	BS EE
88	MA COMM
65	MS CS
65	PHD CS

Now, inserting a new degree for Chu requires only inserting a single row into the EDUCATION table.

Second Normal Form

Second Normal Form: a relation is said to be in second normal form if and only if it is in first normal form and every non-key attribute of the relation is fully functionally dependent on the primary key.

SID	SNAME	City	Status
4	Smith	NYC	45
6	Liu	DC	65
7	Chen	NYC	45
9	Jones	LA	22

Second Normal Form was also formulated by Ted Codd.[15] This supplier table shows supplier IDs, the name for each supplier and the city where the supplier is located and the status of the city (which might be, say, a tax rate or an average temperature). The functional dependency diagram below shows how supplier ID and supplier name functionally determine each other jointly, and they jointly determine city and city determines status.

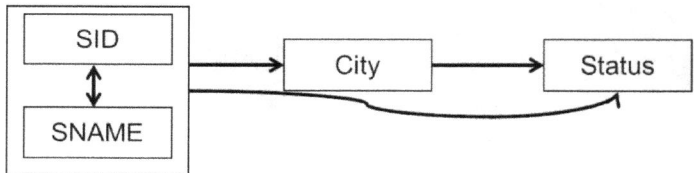

Figure 15. FDD for 2NF

---

[15] E. F. Codd, *Further normalization of the data base relational model.* Presented at Courant Computer Science Symposia Series 6, "Data Base Systems," New York City, Mary 24-25, 1971. IBM Research Report RJ909 (August 31, 1971). Republished in Randall J. Rustin (ed.), Data Base Systems: *Courant Computer Science Symposia Series 6.* Prentice-Hall, 1972.

Because STATUS is a characteristic of the city, and each supplier is associated with only one city, each supplier will have the same status for every part from that supplier. Thus, we say that STATUS is determined *transitively* by the composite key SID and SNAME.

Now let's look at this example from the standpoint of Roberts's Rules.

Rule One requires that a table be about only one entity type. However, we see that STATUS is not about the supplier; It's the status of the city. Looking at the status attribute from a fact-based point of view, we see that STATUS doesn't tell us anything more about the supplier; it tells us something about the city. This table is not strictly about a single entity type; it's about two entity types and does not comply with Roberts's Rule One.

Rule Two says that each fact should be represented only once. EMP shows that Smith and Chen are both located in New York City. Because New York City has status 45, the fact of New York City's status is shown twice. Indeed, if there are many suppliers within a city, the status of that city will be displayed many times in this table. Roberts's Rule Two has been violated, as well as Rule One. Although Rule One and Rule Two take very different points of view we see that in many cases compliance in violation of Rule One and Rule Two go together.

There are anomalies with this structure. If the status of a city changes, that city's status must be changed throughout the supplier table. A single change in value of one fact may require many updates to the table.

From this example, we can say that second normal form does not guarantee compliance with Rule One or Rule Two because it permits transitive dependencies.

Third Normal Form

Third Normal Form: *A relation is said to be in third normal form if and only if it is in second normal form and there are no transitive dependencies.*

Third normal form can be viewed as an improvement in the sense of "aboutness" from second normal form. By eliminating transitive dependencies, third normal form makes a relation more compliant with Roberts's Rule One and Roberts's Rule Two.

We can convert the previous example that was in second normal form into third normal form by moving the information about city and status into a separate table of information about cities. Our one second normal form table will now be represented as two tables in the database as shown here:

SUPPLIER

SID	SNAME	City
4	Smith	NYC
6	Liu	DC
7	Chen	NYC
9	Jones	LA

SID

SID	SNAME
4	Smith
6	Liu
7	Chen
9	Jones

These two tables are described by these FDDs, one for each table:

```
┌─────────────────────────┐
│  ┌───────────────┐      │
│  │     SID       │      │        ┌───────────────┐
│  └───────────────┘      │───────▶│     City      │
│         ↕               │        └───────────────┘
│  ┌───────────────┐      │
│  │    SNAME      │      │
│  └───────────────┘      │
└─────────────────────────┘
```

```
┌───────────────┐              ┌───────────────┐
│     City      │─────────────▶│    Status     │
└───────────────┘              └───────────────┘
```

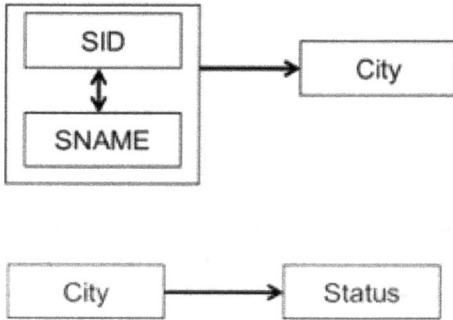

Third Normal Form refines the notion of *aboutness* beyond the restrictions of second normal form. By eliminating transitive dependencies, Third Normal Form prohibits attributes that are about a different entity and not about the entity that's described by the relation.

Boyce-Codd Normal Form
Boyce-Codd Normal form, also introduced by Ted Codd[16], fixes a third normal form anomaly. Because the definition of third normal form deals only with non-key attributes, it was discovered that if there are composite primary keys that overlap, then they might behave badly and introduce anomalies. Here's an example of that behavior, using Chris Date's suppliers and parts example:

---

[16] E. F. Codd, *Recent investigations into relational data base systems. IBM Research Report RJ1385 (April 23, 1974). Republished in* Proc. 1974 Congress (Stockholm, Sweden, 1974) New York, N.Y.: North-Holland (1974).

S#	SNAME	P#	QTY
1	Acme	65	788
2	Chen	34	76
3	Jones	65	34

Here is the functional dependency diagram for this example:

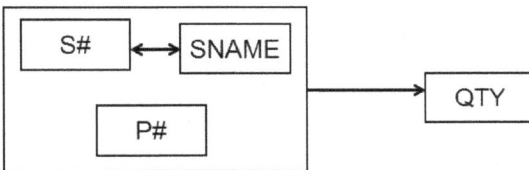

This example table shows the quantity of each part that we have from each supplier. For each supplier, we have a supplier number and the supplier name. The supplier number and the supplier name determine each other, and the supplier identity along with the part number determines the quantity of that part from that supplier that we have an inventory.

In this example, it's easy to say that if Acme supplies more than one part, then if Acme changes its company name, we will have to make multiple changes of the name in this table. That's an update anomaly. We note also that Roberts's Rule Two is not followed; the fact that supplier number one is

Acme can be represented in this table many times if Acme supplies many different parts.

This table is in Third Normal Form. The functional dependency diagram shows that the non-key attributes which are here only quantity are fully functionally dependent on the primary key, which is a composite key. So we see that even in a relation that is in third normal form, we can still have anomalies.

Boyce-Codd normal form eliminates the possible anomalies of third normal form. Here's its definition:

A table is said to be in Boyce-Codd normal form if and only if every determinant is a key.

This definition is a easier to understand if you insert the word "complete" in front of the word "key". The definition of Boyce-Codd normal form requires that every attribute that determines another attribute, or every composite attribute that determines another attribute, must be a complete key. In other words, a single attribute cannot determine another attribute unless it's a complete primary key. In the example above, both supplier number and supplier name determine each other, but neither of them is a complete key. Therefore, the example is not in Boyce-Codd normal form.

To convert this relation to Boyce-Codd normal form, we break it into two tables. One of them shows the relationship of supplier number and supplier name. The other shows the relationship between supplier

our identity part number and quantity. Here are the
two new tables:

S#	P#	QTY
1	65	788
2	34	76
3	65	34

S#	SNAME
1	Acme
2	Chen
3	Jones

and here are the functional dependency diagrams for
these tables:

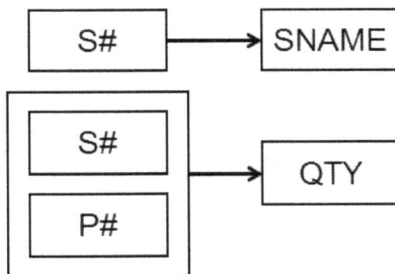

A table in Third Normal Form but not in Boyce-Codd
Normal Form shows anomalous behavior that is very
much like a relation that's in second normal form but
not third normal form. In both situations, we could
say that there is information in the relation that is not
strictly about the entity type that is described by the
relation. In the example, the entity type that's
described by the relation is a single part
manufactured by a single manufacturer. Because the
original table had both supplier number and supplier
name, there is some information here that is really

about the supplier rather than about the part. That's like the situation that we saw with transitive dependencies.

Fourth Normal Form

Some database textbooks omit fourth normal form on the basis that it is not encountered in practice and is of only academic interest. In my experience, this is incorrect; that view is supported by a survey of forty organization's databases. Nine of them were found to contain data of fourth normal form[17].

Fourth normal form was introduced by Ronald Fagin in 1977[18]. It is based on the concept of *multi-valued dependency*, a generalization of functional dependency (see page 96), which is a constraint between the values of two attributes in a table.

A *multi-valued attribute* is an attribute of an entity type that can have more than one value for an instance of that entity type. For example, today each person may have multiple telephone numbers, so *telephone number* would be a multi-valued attribute. Examples of other common multi-valued attributes are email address and even home address, for people might have more than one residence.

---

[17] Margaret S. Wu, The practical need for fourth normal form, ACM SIGCSE Bulletin, **24,** 1 (March 1992), pp. 19-23. https://doi.org/10.1145/135250.134515
[18] Ronald Fagin (September 1977), Multivalued dependencies and a new normal form for relational databases, *ACM Transactions on Database Systems* **2** (1) 267.

An MVD exists when there are at least three attributes (such as COURSE#, TEACHER, BOOK) in a table, and for a value of COURSE# there is a well-defined set of values for TEACHER, and those values are independent of those for BOOK. That is, for each value of COURSE# there is a set of values for TEACHER, determined by only COURSE#.

The notion of MVD is a generalization of functional dependency (FD); the notion of determining a single value in an FD is generalized into determining a set of values. Thus, every FD is also an MVD, while not every MVD is an FD.

An MVD results in significant redundancy in how data is stored. Consider the example below, which shows students, the sports they play and the musical instruments they play:

SID	Sport	Instrument
87	Soccer	Saxophone
87	Tennis	Violin
87	Soccer	Violin
87	Tennis	Saxophone

Fourth Normal Form: a table is said to be in fourth normal form if and only if it is in third normal form and it has no more than one multivalued dependency.

Consider the example above, a table used to track student IDs along with the sports the student in plays, and musical instruments that the student plays. Each student might play multiple sports, and each student might play multiple instruments.

The example shows the entries for just one student, with student ID 87. This (very active!) student plays two sports, soccer and tennis, and two instruments, saxophone and violin. The table has two multivalued dependencies, as illustrated by this functional dependency diagram:

In order to properly represent the data in this table with two multivalued dependencies, some duplication has been necessary. We want to be able to find student 87 if someone searches for a student who plays soccer and the saxophone. Thus, each value of the sport MVD must be shown along with each value of the instrument MVD to provide the correct result for a query involving a sport and an instrument. This introduces an insert anomaly, because each fact will need to be inserted more than once, as well as similar anomalies for updates and deletes.

Now let's convert this example to Fourth Normal Form. Since Fourth Normal Form allows us to have only one MVD per table, we need to divide this table into two, each with a single MVD. We create one table that shows all the sports each student plays and another table showing the instruments that each student plays. It looks like this:

SID	SPORT
87	SOCCER
87	TENNIS

SID	INSTRUMENT
87	SAXOPHONE
87	VIOLIN

The functional dependency diagrams for these two tables show one multivalued dependency in each table:

```
┌─────────┐
│   SID   │─ MVD →┌──────────────┐
└─────────┘       │  Instrument  │
                  └──────────────┘

┌─────────┐
│   SID   │─ MVD →┌──────────┐
└─────────┘       │  Sport   │
                  └──────────┘
```

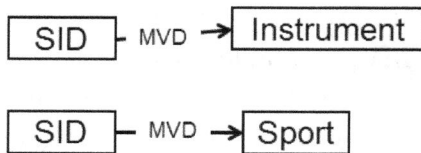

3.9 Roberts's Rules and Normal Forms

In the discussion above, with each normal form we talked about how it corresponded to Roberts's Rules. Now let's turn things around and look at each of Roberts's Rules from the standpoint of normal forms.

Rule One

Rule One requires that each row must be about only a single entity type, so it prohibits a single row from presenting information about two different entity types. In terms of functional dependencies, Rule One is requiring every non-key attribute to be fully functionally dependent on the primary key, because functional dependence and "aboutness" are the same.

It is also easy to see that Rule One prohibits transitive functional dependencies, since a transitive dependency involves an attribute that's "about" a different entity type. Thus, Rule One compliance requires 3NF.

In the case of overlapping composite keys, we could say that Rule One prohibits the sort of behavior in the example table on page 108 that is not in BCNF, because the table could be said to contain information about the supplier, not just about the entity type that intended to be described.

Thus, Rule One, interpreted strictly, requires a table to be in Boyce-Codd normal form.

With regard to 4NF, a table could have two multi-value dependencies with every attribute shown about only a single entity type, so Rule One does not require 4NF.

Rule Two
Rule Two requires that each fact be represented only once. What circumstances cause a fact to be represented more than once? One cause would be a transitive dependency—so Rule Two disallows transitive dependencies, therefore requiring 3NF. However, a table not in BCNF can represent the same fact more than once, so Rule Two also required BCNF.

What about Rule Two and 4NF? A table not in 4NF that has more than one multi-value dependency will have some facts represented more than once, so it will violate Rule 2. Thus, Rule 2 requires 4NF.

Rule Three
Rule Three, that each row must be stored in only one table, and rows cannot move from one table to another, is outside the defined normal forms, which deal with only a single table. The normal forms discussed here have no parallel in Rule Three, which should always be followed, for simplicity of programming and reduction of the difficulty of

software maintenance. Rule 3 adds value beyond
normalization to the data model.

Rule Four

Rule Four, that specifies how repeated values are to
be treated, is related to 4NF, because a repeated value
(or group of values) is a multi-value dependency.
4NF requires that each multi-valued dependency
have a separate table, and so does Rule Four.

3.10 Denormalization

A normalized database is less likely to need changes
in structure as the programs that access it are changed
in response to changes in the processes that those
programs support.   It's evident, though, that
normalization tends to increase the number of tables,
so querying a normalized database will require more
joins that would be needed for an unnormalized
database.   One might expect a normalized database
to provide poorer performance than an unnormalized
database.

However, that view is not correct! The data model
referenced by application programs is an abstraction,
and not necessarily how the data is physically stored.
Normalization may not affect performance at all if
the larger number of tables of the normalized
database are stored in a way to make joins run
quickly.

Consider our EMP – DEPT example, and the
occasional need to join the two tables. For a join on
DEPTNO, the database system must find all the rows
with matching values of DEPTNO in the two tables.

Suppose that each row of DEPT was stored in the same physical disk records as the rows of EMP that for employees in that department. Then a join of EMP and DEPT could be carried out with a scan of the DEPT table, picking up the associated rows of EMP along the way.

This method of storage can be called pre-joining of tables. Oracle calls such an arrangement a *cluster,* created by the CREATE CLUSTER statement in SQL.

Creating a cluster changes the physical arrangement of the database but does not change the view of tables seen by the application program. This allows the database to be tuned for performance without changing programs.

In the early days of relational database, when algorithms were less efficient and computers were many orders of magnitude slower, denormalization needed to be the database administrator's toolkit, and was used from time to time to meet performance requirements. Today's hardware and software enables a database system to operate at performance levels that greatly reduce the need for denormalization. In addition, SQL statements that change the database physical structure to tune for performance without changing the application program view of the database further reduce the need for denormalization.

In practice, I have seen denormalization used only in a negative way. If programmers are in charge of the data model for a project and don't understand normalization (and many don't), they use the statement "We denormalized for performance" when asked about their use of normalization.

The appropriate approach is to start with a normalized data model, and if there are performance concerns, adjust the physical data structure to achieve required performance. Only if that effort fails should a denormalized data model be considered.

What is Denormalization?
Denormalization is usually the introduction of redundant data to improve performance of some operation. This generally comes at the cost of poorer performance of another operation.

In addition, redundant data can become inconsistent data. The initial designers of an application will understand how to insert new data and update data when there are multiple representations of the same fact. While programming will be more complex, it can be done. Maintenance programmers who work on the application later may have trouble updating all copies of the data, leading to problems that are hard to diagnose and repair.

Overall, denormalization is a compromise, where increased programming complexity and poorer performance of one operation is traded off for increased performance of some critical operation.

Consider this simple example of two tables. The first is the familiar EMP table; the second is a table of contact methods, that shows, for each employee, all the contact methods for that employee. In schema form, the table definitions are the following:

> EMP(EMPNO,   ENAME,   JOB,   SAL,
> DEPTNO)
> CONTACTMETHOD(EMPNO,   METHOD,
> CONTACTID)

This schema is normalized. It allows each employee to have any number of types of contact methods. An employee could have five different phone numbers, for example. This allows for complete freedom and generality regarding contact methods for each employee.

In order to find a method to contact an employee, a join must be performed. One way to denormalize so that a join is not required is to store all the data in a single table, restricting the contact methods to one email address and one phone number. The schema for the new database is as follows:

> EMP(EMPNO,   ENAME,   JOB,   SAL,
> DEPTNO, PHONE, EMAIL)

Any employee's contact information can now be found without a join; what has been sacrificed here is the ability to store multiple phone numbers and multiple email addresses for each employee. This table is still normalized.

But now suppose the decision is made to keep the single table for performance but allow for two phone numbers and two email addresses per employee. The new EMP table would have this schema representation:

EMP(EMPNO, ENAME, JOB, SAL, DEPTNO, PHONE1, PHONE2, EMAIL1, EMAIL2)

This table violates Rule 3, because the attributes PHONE and EMAIL have been found to be of cardinality greater than one, but the design is not insensitive to cardinality. If either of these values has cardinality greater than one, then all value starting with the third can't be appropriately stored in the table.

In this case, the inability to store a second value for email address or phone number that was present with the first change has been relieved. The cost will be more complex programming, because a SELECT statement will retrieve both values for EMAIL and for PHONE, and the application will have to provide them, in addition to the limitation of two values for each.

The most important techniques for denormalization are these:

Duplicate databases

Duplicate tables

Split tables

Pre-joined tables

Repeating groups across rows

Pre-calculation of derived results

Duplicate Databases

If high-performance retrieval is a priority and the database does not have to be instantaneously correct, duplicate databases may provide a useful option that requires little programming effort and no changes to the data model.

One database is updated, and then one or more copies are used for retrieval. Most database products have a feature available called replication services, that will automatically copy updates from one table to another or from one database to another.

Note that the duplicate database will not be identical to the primary database; it will lag it by whatever time replication services takes to make the copy. Thus, this approach is not appropriate for retrieval of real-time information such as current bank balances.

Duplicate Tables
If all reads can be directed to a single table, then a duplicate table can be employed. Replication services can be used to automatically update the duplicate table. Similarly, here, too, the duplicate data will not be perfectly synchronized with the original data.

Split Tables
There are two types of split tables: vertical splits and horizontal splits.

With a vertical split, attributes are divided between two tables, with the primary key put into both tables. Thus, with a vertical split each table will have the same number of rows.

The vertical split approach is particularly attractive if one group of applications accesses some columns, and another group of applications accesses other columns. This can be a practical approach.

With a horizontal split, rows are divided between the two tables, with the choice of table usually decided by the primary key value. Each of the two tables will have the same columns as the pre-split table.

Every application that accesses the two tables now must incorporate the denormalization logic and decide which of the split tables to access. Search when the primary key is not known now must be two SELECT statements and a UNION operation to consolidate their results, adding a performance penalty. The horizontal split approach provides limited benefits and is not usually practical.

In addition, the use of table partitioning can provide the performance benefit of a horizontal split without changing the data model. The Oracle statement CREATE PARTITION can be used to divide a very large table or index into separate partitions without changing the data model.

Pre-joined tables
If joins of some tables are performed very frequently, and there is a performance problem, then those two tables can be pre-joined and combined into a single

table. For example, the EMP and DEPT example tables can be combined in this way.

> EMP(EMPNO, DEPTNO, ENAME, JOB, SAL)
> DEPT(DEPTNO, DNAME, LOC)

Can be pre-joined into

> EMPDEPT(EMPNO, ENAME, JOB, SAL, DEPTNO, DNAME, LOC)

Note that this table is no longer about a single entity type, and if any of the information about a department changes, then many rows will need to be changed. However, employee and department information can now be related without performing a join.

Clustering the two tables using the CREATE CLUSTER statement can provide the same performance benefit without changing the data model.

Repeating groups across rows
This is the technique that was used in the first example above of denormalization, dealing with multiple email addresses and phone numbers (see page 120). Multiple columns are allocated for occurrences of repeating groups. This approach introduces additional programming complexity, since the application must deal with the anomaly that two different column names are being used for the same attribute. Also, the cardinality of the repeating attribute cannot be greater than the number of repeats that are built into the table. If the decision is made

that an employee can have a maximum of two degrees, what happens with the first employee with three degrees?

This is an example of a normalized structure for employees and degrees:

■■■I

EMPNO	ENAME
20	WU
30	SMITH
40	CHEN

EMPNO	DEGREE	MAJOR
20	MS	COMPUTER APPS
20	BS	EE
30	BS	HISTORY
30	JD	LAW

Figure 16. Normalized Employees and Degrees

Denormalized with repeating groups across rows produces this structure:

EMPNO	ENAME	DEG1	MAJ1	DEG2	MAJ2
20	WU	BS	EE	MS	COMPUTER APPS
30	SMITH	BS	HISTORY	JD	LAW
40	CHEN				

Figure 17. Repeating Groups Across Rows

This approach introduces considerable programming complexity. Consider how to program an update of Smith's JD in LAW to a JD in Law Management.

Pre-calculation of derived results

If calculated results are needed frequently, the calculated results can be calculated when the data is stored and updated, so that it does not have to be calculated when retrieved. Here is the EMP table with total compensation pre-calculated:

EMPNO	ENAME	JOB	DEPTNO	SAL	COMM	COMP
20	SMITH	PRES	3	150		150
30	CHEN	DEPTNO	3	130		130
40	LIU	SALES MGR	5	100		100
40	JONES	SALES REP	5	20	30	50

Figure 18. Precalculated Total Compensation

Whenever SAL or COMM is updated, COMM must be recalculated. This will also slow updates. However, retrieval of COMP will be faster, because it will not have to be calculated at the time of retrieval.

Summary

Denormalization can make some operations faster, while making others slower, and potentially introducing additional programing complexity. While short-term performance gains can be achieved through denormalization, the added programming complexity that is involved as well as the future limitations in data model evolution can introduce considerable risk into a programming project.

Before denormalization is considered, a normalized data model should be designed and efforts made to achieve the needed performance by tuning physical data structures, exploiting the data independence of the relational approach, without denormalizing the data model.

Chapter 4   Data Modeling

4.1   Introduction

A relational database models some environment outside the computer. The database is a collection of independent tables with fixed structure but varying content, with each table modeling one entity type in the problem space. Each row of the table models a single occurrence, or instance, of that entity type.

Before we can write applications to access a relational database, first we must establish the database. That requires us to decide which tables to include as well as the columns for each table.

Since each table models one entity type, we must choose the entity types to be modeled. Sometimes the choice is obvious, such as the example of departments and employees. Other times the choice may be more difficult, such as an accounting system. For an excellent data model for an accounting system, see David Hay's book.[19] When you begin work, the entity types may not be obvious.

When I first approached the problem of needing to develop a data model, my first inquiry was toward data modeling tools that were being available, expecting that these tools would help

---

[19] David C. Hay, Data Model Patterns, Conventions of Thought. 1996, Dorset House Publishing, ISBN 0-932633-29-3, 268 pages.

one decide which tables and columns to include in a database. Unfortunately, that's not the case; the tools simply help draw diagrams that can be used to communicate about entity types and relationships. Such communication is important to develop an understanding of the data model, so the tools are useful. However, they aren't design tools, they are really data model drawing tools.

4.2   Data Model Diagrams

Peter Chen introduced the E-R notation for diagramming data models. Chen diagrams are easy to understand and are excellent in the early stages of analysis, when you are building your understanding of the problem.[20]

When we are building a data model diagram, there are three types of information to represent on the diagram:

- entity types
- attributes
- relationships between entity types

A Chen diagram shows all of these in a way that is easy to understand. In fact, a good method for developing a data model is to meet with users of the data, and, in meetings with them, develop Chen diagrams that describe the entity types, attributes and relationships. End-users who work

---

[20] Chen, Peter P. The entity-relationship model—toward a unified view of data. *ACM Transactions on Database Systems*, 1, 1 (March 1976), 9-36.

with the data on a day-to-day basis typically have very good understanding of this information and can be helpful in their analysis of the problem if Chen diagrams are used.

Entities

There are two types of entities: strong entities and weak entities. A strong entity has an independent existence, while an instance of a weak entity depends for its existence on a corresponding instance of a strong entity. *Employee* is an example of a strong entity, and *dependent* an example of a weak entity.

A strong entity is represented by a rectangle; a week entity is represented by a double rectangle, as shown below:

Strong Entity

Weak Entity

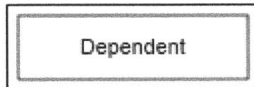

Figure 19. Entity Types

Each entity is characterized by attributes. Attributes are shown on a Chen diagram as ovals, connected to their entity with a solid line. The attribute that is key is underlined in the diagram, as shown below:

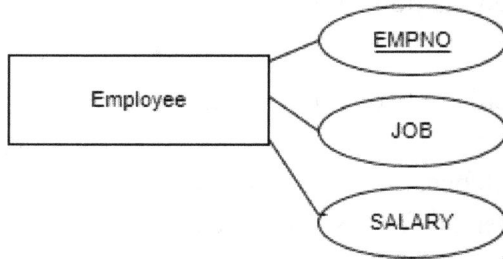

Figure 20. Attributes

Relationships

A relationship is an association between two entity types, for example:

- a CUSTOMER might *place* a CUSTOMER ORDER
- an EMPLOYEE might *take* a CUSTOMER ORDER
- a STUDENT might *enroll* in a COURSE
- a COURSE is *taught* by a FACULTY MEMBER

Entity types above are in upper case, relationships in italics. Sometimes entity types are described as being nouns, while relationships are verbs. A relationship is given a name and is represented by a diamond–shaped symbol that connects with the entity types involved. The figure below shows employee working for department:

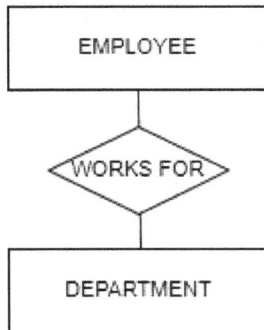

Figure 21. Employee Works for Department

A relationship with a weak entity is portrayed similarly:

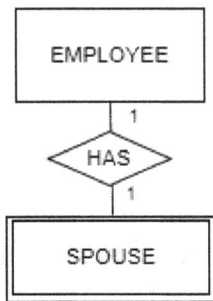

Figure 22. Relationship with Weak Entity

A relationship can be categorized by its *cardinality*, its *degree* and its *optionality*.

The *cardinality* of the relationship can be one-many, many-many, or one-one. A one-many relationship is a hierarchy, where a single instance of one entity type can be associated with multiple instances of another entity type, such as our example of departments and employees, where each department can be associated with many employees.

For a many-many relationship, on each side of the relationship a single instance can be associated with multiple instances on the other side. Students and courses or an example of a many-many relationship. Each student can be enrolled in multiple courses, and each course can enroll multiple students.

A one-one relationship is unusual. It occurs primarily as a relationship between a strong entity and a week entity, such as *employee* and spouse (presuming that local laws permit only one spouse). Often during analysis, a one-one relationship may appear to be present when there is not a weak entity type involved. When that happens, consider whether the two entity types involved in the one-one relationship are best modeled as a single entity type.

The figure below shows example relationships of different cardinality. In a Chen diagram, the cardinality is indicated with the number 1 or letters on both sides of the relationship.

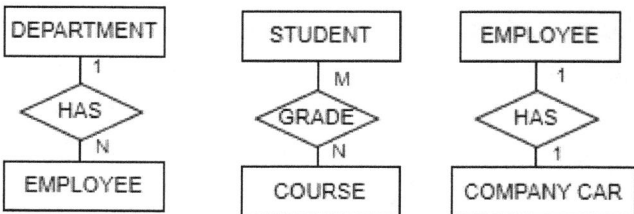

Figure 23. Cardinality of Relationships

The number of entity types participating in a
relationship is called the *degree* of the
relationship. The example shown above all have
degree two. However, it's possible for just a
single entity type to be involved in a relationship,
or more than two entity types.

A relationship involving only a single entity type
is called a recursive relationship, and can be used
to represent a repeated hierarchy, as shown below.
This hierarchy can be continued to any number of
levels, without changing the data model:

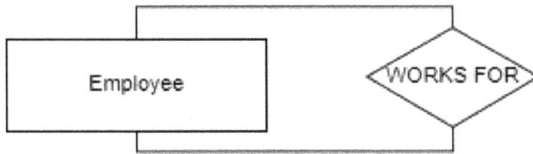

Figure 24. Recursive Relationship

Relationships of degree higher than two are not
unusual. An example of such a relationship is
students, teachers, and courses. A student can
take multiple courses, a teacher can teach multiple
courses, and a course can be taught by multiple
teachers and enroll multiple students. The Chen
diagram below illustrates this relationship of
degree three:

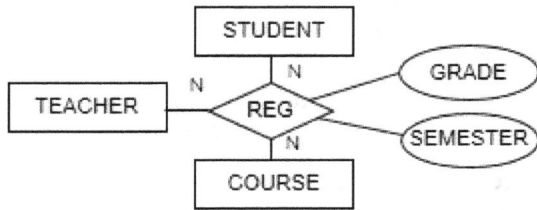

Figure 25. Ternary Relationship

Finally, relationships can have differing requirements for participation, called *optionality*. Optionality is also indicated on Chen diagrams. If participation is required, a short line is drawn perpendicular to the relationship line is drawn, near the entity symbol. If participation is optional, then a small "o" is placed between the relationship line and the symbol. This is illustrated by the figure below, where the example of Figure 23 has been expanded by the addition of optionality:

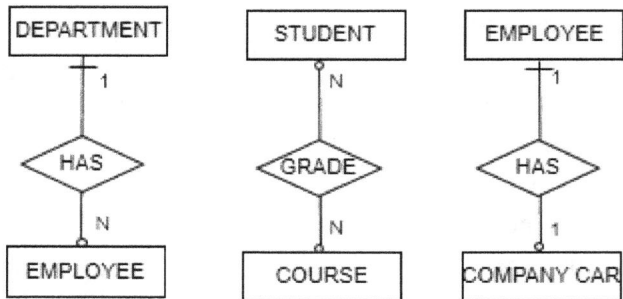

Figure 26. Optionality

4.3   Weak Entity Types

Most entity types that you will encounter are strong entity types, that exist independently from other entity types. However, there are also two other entity types, associative entities and subtype entities.

A strong entity type always has a unique identifier that identifies each instance of that entity type. For example, the identifier for employee might be social security number. Each employee would have a Social Security number unique to that employee. On the other hand, dependent, a week entity type dependent on employee, could have its own social security number but it's also essential that we be able to associate the dependent with an employee. Therefore, dependent would a composite key of the employee's Social Security number and the dependent's Social Security number. The entity type upon which the week entity type depends is called the *identifying owner*.

The figure below shows a Chen diagram for a strong entity type and its relationship with a weak entity type:

Figure 27. Weak Entity Type and Identifying Entity Type

An associative entity type is a many-to-many relationship, identified as a diamond in a Chen ERD. In general, an associative entity type will have attributes of its own. The key of the associative entity type is the key of its associated strong entity types. The figure below shows an associative relationship between student and course. They are associated by the relationship created when the student registers for a course.

Figure 28. Associative Relationship Entity Type

In this relationship, each course is associated with zero or more students, and each student is associated with zero or more courses. Permitting the zero value allows a student to be inserted even though they are not yet associated with a course, and similarly for courses.

4.4   Types and Supertypes

A subtype is a subgrouping of the entities in an entity type that is meaningful to the organization. For example, STUDENT could be an entity type at a university, with subtypes GRADUATE STUDENT and UNDERGRADUATE STUDENT. In this case, STUDENT is called the supertype. A supertype is a generic entity type that has a relationship with one or more subtypes.

It can be useful to consider a supertype that includes several entity types as subtypes. If several entity types share common attributes, relationships or integrity constraints, these can all be placed in the supertype, so that they are represented only once for all the entity types. The subtypes are used for the attributes, relationships and integrity constraints that are unique to each subtype. The result is a data model and queries that are simplified and can have better control over integrity.

For example, consider a company that has three different classes of employees, and their attributes:

> Hourly employee—EMPNO, ENAME, DATE_HIRED, HOURLY_RATE

> Salaried employee—EMPNO, ENAME, DATE_HIRED, ANNUAL_SALARY, STOCK_OPTION

> Contract consultant—EMPNO, ENAME, DATE_HIRED, CONTRACT_NO, BILLING_RATE

In this situation, here are three ways to construct the data model:

Define a single entity type, EMPLOYEE. This might seem to be the simple and obvious approach; however, EMPLOYEE would need to include all the attributes for all three types of employees. For any given employee, only the attributes of one of the three types of employees would be relevant, so each row would have several null values. Programs processing this data would have additional complexity to deal with the variations.

Define three different entity types. This approach fails to take advantage of the common attributes of the three kinds of employees. Users would need to be careful to choose the right entity type when using the system.

Define a supertype, EMPLOYEE, with subtypes HOURLY, SALARIED, and CONSULTANT. This approach recognizes the common attributes and has just a single column for each common attribute, yet it recognizes the distinct properties of each kind of employee.

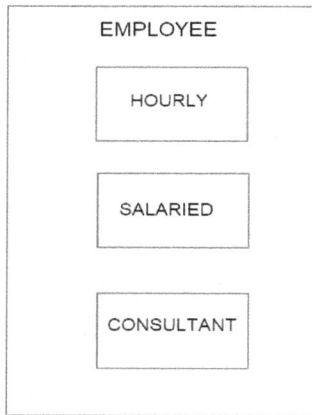

Figure 29. EMPLOYEE Supertype and Subtypes

Here is a schema definition that shows how this data model could be implemented:

EMPLOYEE(EMPLOYEEID,   FNAME,   LNAME, ADDRESS, HOMEPHONE)
HOURLY(EMPLOYEEID,HIREDATE, HOURLYRATE)
SALARIED(EMPLOYEEID,HIREDATE, ANNUAL RATE)

Subtypes can be either mutually exclusive, called disjoint, or overlapping, called inclusive.

For disjoint subtypes, an entity instance can be in only one subtype

For overlapping subtypes, an entity instance can be in two or more subtypes

Usually we use only disjoint subtypes, that also follow the completeness constraint: all instances of a subtype must be represented in the supertype.

Here is another example, that is commonly used for company databases with information about people and organizations:

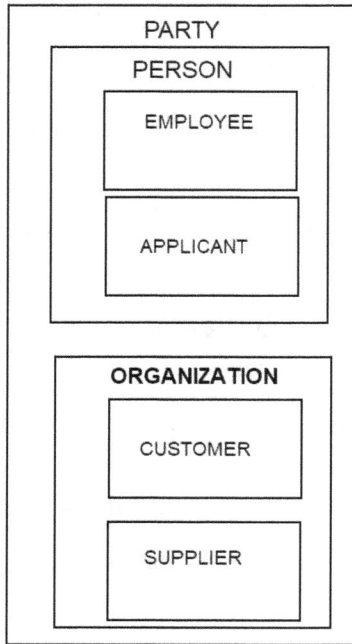

Figure 30. PARTY Supertype and Subtypes

In this case, the subtypes of PARTY will not share many attributes, or perhaps not any, so PARTY may have as its only attribute the key. The subtypes of PERSON will share some attributes, so PERSON will have several attributes, as will ORGANIZATION.

Here is a schema definition implementing this data model:

PARTY(PARTYID)
PERSON(PARTYID, FNAME, MI, LNAME, DOB, POB)
EMPLOYEE(PARTYID, DATEHIRED, SALARY, JOB, DEPTNO)
APPLICANT(PARTYID, DATEAPPLIED, STATUS)
ORGANIZATION(PARTYID, ORGNAME, CITY, STATE, ZIP)
CUSTOMER(PARTYID, DATEOFFIRSTORDER, DATEOFLASTORDER,
SUPPLIER(PARTYID, DATEOFFIRSTORDER, DATEOFLASTORDER, Y

The use of supertypes and subtypes can simplify the representation of relationships in the database. A relationship can be with a subtype, or, if all the subtypes of a common supertype share a relationship, then that relationship can be shown with a supertype. This can significantly reduce the number of relationships that are represented in the database.

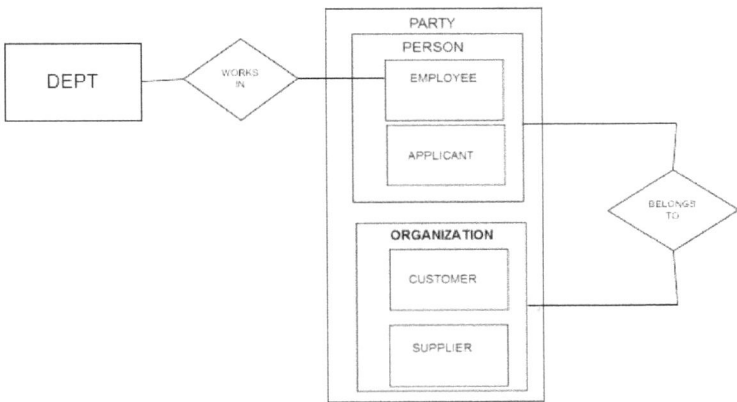

Figure 31. Supertypes, Subtypes and relationships

The figure above shows how employees can be assigned to departments, where EMPLOYEE is the only entity type with a relationship to DEPARTMENT. However, in the case of the BELONGS TO relationship, either an employee or an applicant can belong to a customer or a supplier, so the relationship in this case is between the supertypes ORGANIZATION and PERSON.

4.5   Natural and Generated Keys
A natural key is a candidate key that occurs in the data, that uniquely identifies rows. A generated key is a value that is generated at the time data is inserted into the database, that did not occur outside the database.

In some organizations, if you look at an ERD for a large project, you'll see that every table has a column whose name ends in ID. If you ask about this column, you'll be told that it's the key, that relational database requires each row to have a unique identifier, so they provide a unique identifier for each table.

That view, although common, is incorrect. In fact, it reflects a misunderstanding of relational database, and if you use this approach, you will not realize some of the important benefits of relational database.

It is true that every row of each table must be unique. However, this is necessary because each row describes a different instance of some entity type that occurs outside the database. If two rows are identical, then the database doesn't have enough information to distinguish the two instances in the real world. The way to correct this problem is to find additional attributes of the entity type that will distinguish these instances. If a generated key is used to distinguish them, the database still won't have enough information to tell the two instances apart.

When to Not Use a Generated Key
Note that if a table is in third normal form, then every non-key attribute of the table must be fully functionally dependent on the primary key. Which means that the primary key uniquely identifies instances of the entity type, and hence also identifies the row that describes each instance. This means that if a table is in third or higher normal form, that it does not need a generated key to have a unique identifier.

Looking at it from the standpoint of the real-world problem that is modeled by the database, each instance of an entity type must be different from all the other entity types. That's why we track them as individuals. Therefore, every row is different from every other row without adding another column to it. If the rows we are storing are not unique, then we have not captured enough data about the entity instances. If two rows of the table may be identical unless we add a generated key to them, then we have a fundamental problem – we have not captured enough attributes to distinguish between the two instances. Adding a generated key won't solve that problem.

For example, some new relational database users were researchers who were using the database to store scientific observations made by their instruments. As an experiment progressed, several attributes would be measured and entered into the database. When they retrieved the results of an experiment using a SELECT statement, though, they found that the results would not come back in time order, so they could not ascertain the time sequence of their observations.

Their problem is that they had not included enough attributes to make all the distinctions they needed to make. All they had to do is capture the time of the observation as another attribute, and they could view and process their observations in time sequence, or any other sequence.

Sometimes the claim is made that generated key allows for more flexibility. For example, in an employee table, if we employee number is the primary key, what if we change an employee's employee number? Particularly, what if the employee number is used as a foreign key in other tables throughout the database? Happily, when a foreign key is defined, using CREATE TABLE or ALTER TABLE, the database will handle changes in foreign key values. As part of the definition, with some variations for different database systems, you can choose whether changes in value of a foreign key are allowed, and if allowed if they are propagated to other tables, set to NULL in the other tables, no action is taken, or they are set to some default value in the other tables.

There are benefits to the use of natural keys as the key to a table in a database. Of course, without unnecessary generated keys, tables have fewer columns, and the database is simpler. The database system automatically forces the primary key to be unique, so if the primary key is a value that uniquely identifies entity instances in the real world, then this database constraint corresponds to a real world constraint, and that constraint does not have to be implemented in application code.

When to Use a Generated Key
There are situations where a generated key should be used. If a composite key consists of three or more columns, and it is used frequently as a foreign key, then it will add at least three columns to every table using it as a foreign key. In addition, SQL statements retrieving from those tables will have to mention all these columns. In this case, use of a generated key simplifies programming significantly, so its use is appropriate.

There is another case where a generated key may be needed. Relational database systems generally do not allow for a composite key to have any elements that can be null. This can cause a problem where there is not a single identifier that is shared by all the rows.

For example, if you are designing a table of students, students from the United States will have Social Security numbers, that make excellent keys, but students from other countries may not have Social Security numbers; they may have other identifying national numbers. Thus, while each instance has a unique identifier, they don't share a single common identifier. Two approaches to consider would be:

1. Use identifier type and identifier as two attributes of a composite key. For a U.S.

student, the key would have the value "SSN" for the type, and then the student's SSN as the identifier. For a Chinese student, the two attributes might be "PASSPORT#" and the passport number.
2. Generate a foreign key.

Note that if the second approach is used, the application will need to include code to guarantee uniqueness of identifiers; in the first approach, the database does that automatically through the uniqueness constraint.

4.6   Conversion of an ERD to Relational Tables
The goal of drawing an ERD is to design a relational database. Once the ERD is complete, it's time to convert the ERD into its representation as tables in a database. Happily, there is an algorithm to do this, and most data modeling tools do it automatically.

Entity Types
The rectangles on the ERD are the easiest part. Strong and weak entity types from the ERD, symbolized by rectangles and rectangles with double lines, all become tables in the database, with the attributes identified with each of them, and the key values that have been identified.

Relationships
For one-many relationships, put the identifier of the one with the many. For example, in the employee database, there is a one-many relationship between departments and employees. By including the department number with each employee row, we

have put the identifier of the one with the many. One-many relationships on the ERD do not become database tables.

EMP

EMPNO	ENAME	DEPTNO	JOB	MGR	SAL	COMM
20	SMITH	3	PRES		150	
30	CHEN	3	VPRES	20	120	
40	LIU	5	SALES MGR	30	100	
50	JONES	5	SALES REP	40	20	50

DEPT

DEPTNO	DNAME	LOC
1	FINANCE	NYC
2	MANUF	PHIL
3	HQ	Dc
4	SALES	LA

Figure 32. Example of a One-Many Relationship

Each many-many relationship on the ERD becomes a table, called an associative entity type. The primary key of this table is a composite of the primary keys of all the tables participating in the relationship. In addition, an associative entity type usually has attributes of its own, that become non-key attributes of the table. The figure below illustrates this type of relationship on the ERD:

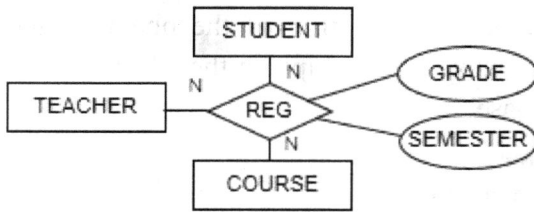

Figure 33. Many-Many Relationship in ERD

Here is how this relationship can be implemented
using   a   database   table:

REG

TeacherID	TNAME	StudentID	STUNAME	COURSE#	Grade	Semes
6566	SMITH	32547	WU	CS35	A	Fall 202
6566	SMITH	32547	WU	CS58	A	Fall 201
73812	ALLEN	65214	JONES	CS76	A	FALL 20
73812	ALLEN	65214	JONES	CS58	B	SPRING

Figure 34. implementation of Many-Many Relationship

One-one relationships between a strong entity and a
weak entity are often valid. Store the identity of the
identifying (strong) instance with the weak entity
instance. If the one-one relationship does not involve
a weak entity type, then consider combining the two
entity types into one.

The implementation of subtypes and supertypes as
tables has been covered in the section above.
Attributes that are shared by subtypes and supertypes
are stored with the highest-level entity that shares
them. The root level supertype may have many
attributes, or, particularly if there are many subtypes,
it's only attribute may be the key.

4.7   Data Model Design

Our treatment of data modeling concludes with some thoughts about how to approach the design of the data model. The first time I learned that there were data modeling tools available, I expected that the tools would implement some algorithm for designing a data model. Unfortunately, that's not the case. They should be called data model drawing tools rather than data model design tools.

The textbooks about database are similarly not very helpful. They talk about normalization from a very theoretical point of view, without much discussion of how to apply it or what it means in a practical sense. There is generally no discussion of how to design a data model.

I've observed that many programmers, even those with graduate degrees in computer science, don't know how to approach the data modeling task. Often programmers are responsible for data modeling, and they can make fundamental errors in data modeling that increase programming complexity and delay project completion.

The best way to develop a data model is to start with interviews of end-users who work with the data. They usually know more about the data and its relationships and constraints than the programmers working on the project ever will. A good approach is to meet with users one functional area at a time and draw a Chen notation ERD with them as they describe the data. The basic Chen notation ERD is only three kinds of symbols – rectangles, diamonds, and ovals, which can be understood by end-users.

Using the ERD, you can talk with end-users about what the program must do, then use the ERD to verify with them that needed attributes and relationships have been captured.

If access to functional users isn't available, a similar process can be carried out based on requirements documents. First, identify the entity types and their attributes. Then enumerate the relationships that are involved, and finally draw an ERD and review it for the difficulty of doing the operations the program has to carry out.

Bill Kent, another participant of the IBM research effort on database, identified a useful approach that he called *fact-based analysis*.[21] Kent suggests first enumerating all the facts that are needed to carry out the functions required of the program. Then, for each of the facts, identify the subject of that fact. Then you group the facts by subject and consider the subjects as possible entity types. The next step is to look for relationships among the entity types.

Once a set of entity types and relationships is developed, then review it for normalization, combining one-one relationships into single entities as appropriate, and considering alternatives.

---

[21] Kent, William. Fact-based data analysis and design. The Journal of Systems and Software 4 (1984), 99-121.

4.8   Patterns in Data Models

There are certain patterns that tend to recur in data models. It's useful to be able to recognize them as you build the data model or within the data model once it has been constructed.

The notation used here is what is usually drawn by data modeling tools, called *crow's-foot notation,* to represent cardinality and optionality in relationships. The figure below illustrates a popular use of this notation:

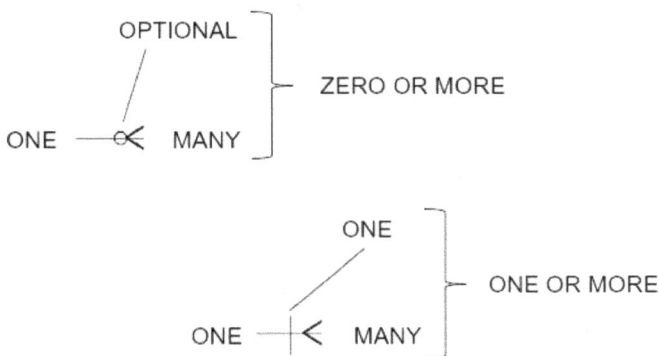

Figure 35. Crow's-Foot Notation

The symbols show constraints on the entity type nearest the symbols. In the figure, the zero followed by the backwards arrow indicates that there are zero or more of the "many" entity instances associated with each instance of the "one" entity. The line indicates that there is one or more instance of the "many" entity type associated with each instance of the "one" entity type.

Association

The first pattern is an association of any type:

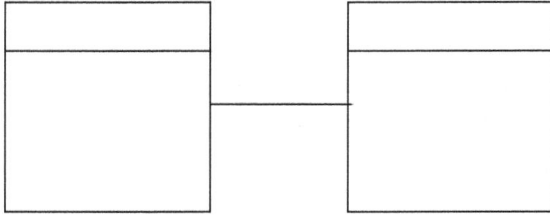

Figure 36. General Association

Type

The second pattern is a type association. The table on the right is called a *type table,* used to require that some column in the table on the left contain one of the values in the type table. A type table usually has just one column. An example would be state abbreviations, where a table is required to contain a valid state abbreviation. The type table would have just one column and 50 rows, listing all the permitted two-letter state abbreviations. An ERD for a typical business application of several hundred tables is likely to have several dozen type tables.

The figure shows a table for businesses, and a type table for business type. This type table would have one column that listed all permitted values for the business type column in the businesses table:

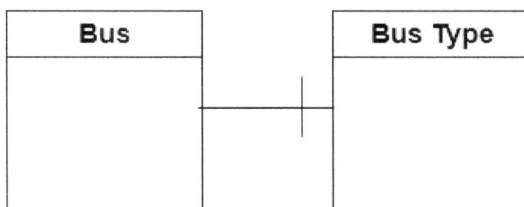

Figure 37. Type Table

Aggregation

Aggregation is a pattern of containment of one collection within another, that can continue for several levels. In aggregation, the "many" cardinality is always on the same side. This can happen in organizations, or in a parts-explosion data model, where a part is combined with other parts to make a subassembly, that combines with other subassemblies, and so on, eventually to make the finished product. The example in the figure below shows aggregation in an organization.

Here, the company is comprised of zero or more divisions, and each division is comprised of zero or more departments. The zero value must be included so that the empty database can be created.

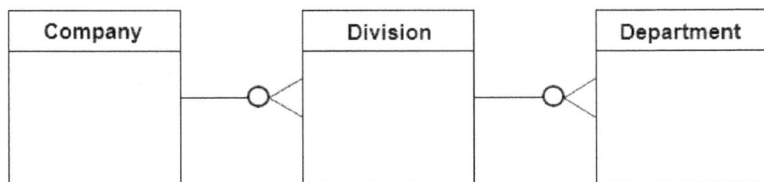

Figure 38. Aggregation

Intersection
The intersection pattern is characterized by a many-many relationship; the "many" cardinality is in the center. A common example is students and courses, where a student takes several courses, and each course enrolls several students. In the figure below, each employee may have several different skills, and each skill is demonstrated by a number of employees:

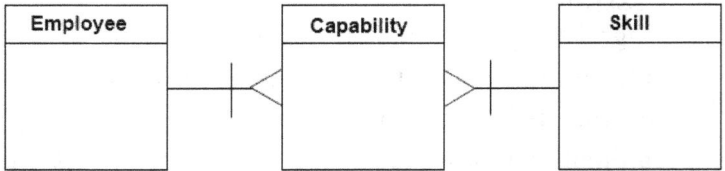

Figure 39. Intersection

Differing Aspects
The pattern of differing aspects of the same entity type is characterized by the "many" cardinality to the outside. This pattern occurs when one entity type has several different attributes that are multi-valued. The example of the figure below shows students who may have more than one address and more than one phone number:

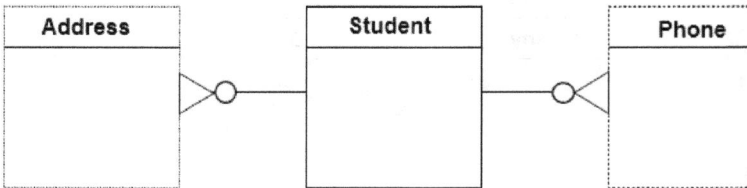

Figure 40. Differing Aspects of the Same

Reflexive

The reflexive association pattern can be used to represent a repeated hierarchy of any depth. This is particularly useful for a hierarchy that is not fixed in height. For a hierarchy that is fixed in height, such as groups, departments and divisions in an organization, programming is simplified by making them explicit in the data model. This figure shows a reflexive association used to represent a "works for" relationship in an organization:

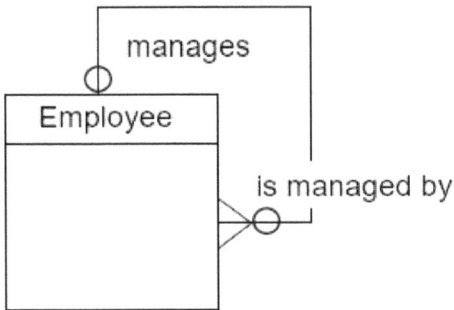

Figure 41. Reflexive Association

Here an employee is managed by zero or more employees (allowing for the president of the company to not have a manager), and an employee manages zero or more other employees.

Inventory

The final pattern is inventory, which falls into two classes. Some items are tracked individually; they have individual identifiers, and often have differences between individuals, such as computers, people, cars, houses, taxpayers and expensive art works. Others are tracked in the aggregate; they tend not to have identifiers, and only quantities are tracked. Examples are pencils, coal, gasoline, water, paint and white blackboard chalk.

II. Database System Operation

Part II presents an overview of how a database system works:

> The major components of a database system, and how they contribute to meeting the overall design goals

> The special optimizations used for on-line analytical processing, that enable fast processing of data structured as star schemas

> Transaction processing techniques that permit database systems to service many processes that are updating the database at once

> Query processing methods to select the fastest approach for the database system to evaluate a query

> The goals and present state of use of database systems in the enterprise

Why should someone who is going to write application programs care about how a database system works? Consider driving a car. You can drive a car perfectly well without knowing how the car works, and we all know some people who do just that. But, for just one example, if you understand how brakes work, and you understand how they wear down over time, you can recognize signs of wear early and get them replaced before there is risk of brake failure. Understanding the basics of how the car works enables you to drive more safely and improves the lifetime of your vehicle.

Similarly, a program that uses a simple SQL statement such as SELECT * FROM EMP; and runs in an environment that does not have a lot of concurrency is not likely to need a lot of attention to just how the database system is processing the query. However, suppose instead the query is a join involving 23 tables, and two of those tables have over 5 million rows? And suppose this is an application that's used internationally by a huge bank, and runs along with concurrent access serving as many as twenty thousand simultaneous users? If that join appears to not be delivering the performance that's needed, clearly an understanding of just how the database system processes the query will be helpful in addressing the performance issues.

There doesn't have to be anything mysterious about the database system and how it works, and that understanding can help you write more effective programs.

Chapter 5   Architecture of a DBMS

5.1   Introduction

This chapter discusses the architecture of a database system. That is, from a high-level view, it describes the components of the database system, what each of them does, and how they work together.

With a relational system, your program interacts with the database system through SQL, which tells the database system what to do, but not how to do it. The database system itself is left to figure out how to process your SQL statement. If you've written a perfectly reasonable SQL statement, and it's clear that the database system is taking a very long time to process the statement, what do you do? Or what if your program performs well in test, but causes a bottleneck when it's run in the production environment? If you have some understanding of what's happening inside the database system, that will help you resolve such issues.

The architecture presented here is not an accurate description of any specific database product. Rather, it's a high-level model of how a relational database system could be constructed, based on the ideas originated with the original IBM papers on relational database, from System R to DB2. All the important database systems in wide use today are based on this IBM work, so they all follow a similar general approach.

When you write a program that accesses the database, the tables accessed may have hundreds of millions of rows. To provide good performance, considerable flexibility in tuning the physical structure of the database for performance has been provided. It's likely that you will never need much of this capability; the intent here is to provide you a foundation for performance tuning of your applications and for further learning.

5.2   Database System Goals

The relational approach to database received its first wide public exposure in 1970 with Ted Codd's landmark article in the Communications of the ACM[22]. His emphasis in that article was on the importance of data independence; that is, isolating programs from knowledge of the detailed structure of how data is stored. Previous database systems used logical relationships that were represented with pointers within the data itself as physical access paths. Thus, when logical relationships changed, programs had to be changed. For complex application systems, changes in the logical structure of the database could cause hundreds or even thousands of application changes. Maintenance could become so difficult that it was impossible to keep an

---

[22] Codd, Edgar F. A relational model of data for large shared data banks. *Communications of the ACM* 13, 6 (Jun 1970), 377-387.

application system up to date as business systems changed.

A byproduct of the relational approach was that the method to process database access now had to be determined by the database system itself instead of by the programmer who was writing application. If the database system made a bad choice, the program might run for minutes or hours when a different method might have had the operation take place in seconds. In fact, early database systems performed so poorly that some experts predicted that it would be impossible for relational database system to ever deliver an acceptable level of performance.

Two factors have worked together to deliver today's relational systems, that have supplanted earlier systems even for transaction processing applications of huge scope:

1. Improved algorithms for deciding how to process SQL statements were developed. These algorithms allowed database systems to make far better choices about how to process requests (see Chapter 8).

2. Moore's Law, that predicts that the performance of computers will double each year, has been valid for more years than expected. Today, we have more computing power in one mobile telephone than would fill a very large computer room in 1970.

This chart illustrates that performance improvement and cost reduction. In 1970, a computer might cost $4 million and have a speed of 12.5 MHz. Today, a computer costing $300 might have a speed of 3600 MHz. The cost per megahertz of performance during that time has dropped from $368,000 to six cents.

	1970	1984	1997	2007	2010	2020
Cost	$4.6 M	$4,000	$1,000	$550	$600	$300
Speed (MHz)	12.5	8.3	166	1600	3000	3600
Cost per MHz	$368,000	$482	$6	$.34	$.10	$.08

Consider the trends in relative costs of computers and programmers. In 1970, the price of a computer might pay the annual salaries of 50 programmers, while today the annual salary of one programmer might pay for 100 computers. 1970 computers were expensive, and programmers were cheap, but today, programmers are expensive, and computers are cheap. It makes sense to use tools like database systems, that cost us machine cycles but make programmers more productive.

5.3   Performance Issues

In the 1970s, performance was the main issue. In early database systems, the data model was tailored to business processes, so that acceptable levels of performance could be achieved. Applications could be built to give good performance, based on a data model highly tailored to the business process. However, when the inevitable changes came in business processes, huge software maintenance burdens were created.

In the mid-1970s, many large companies decided to exploit the growing capability of computers to manage their entire organizations. A number these projects, called management information systems, were undertaken. They involved millions of dollars of programming costs and hundreds of programmers. Their goals were typically the automation and integration of all the business processes of the company. Because of the complexity of the business processes of large companies, building hundreds of computer programs to make up these management information systems was a complex undertaking. In case after case, the teams implementing the systems discovered that the business processes they were attempting to automate were changing faster than they could change their programs to keep up with them.

There were several remarkable news stories where very large US companies, leaders in the business uses of information technology, abandoned these multimillion-dollar efforts when they decided they could never make them work. The underlying culprit was the cost and complexity of software management, particularly when the structure of data showed up in the actual logical structure of application programs.

Of course, relational database systems can't solve all the problems of software engineering, nor can they end all failures of large-scale development efforts. However, these systems and the data independence that they provide are a major reason why complex business systems can be developed and supported today.

With a relational database system, the data model used by programmers is concerned only with the problem that is being solved, and not with issues about how to deliver performance. There are many options regarding the physical structure of the database, but those options can be exercised without changing the data model.

A price is paid for this advantage; relational database system is not nearly as efficient as file structures tailored to a particular application. For a program to access data through a database system, a lot has to happen; and all of that takes machine cycles and elapsed time. A relatively efficient process using a relational database system might take an order of magnitude more processing cycles than a tailored file organization, with the file directly written from the application program. However, the database system allows the application programmer to be much more productive, it allows us to apply computing technology to a much broader and more complex range of problems, so this is a price worth paying.

5.4   How Data Is Stored
Today's database systems typically store all the rows of the table near each other. This is a descendent of the approach used with the first relational systems, that is called the "file per table" approach. Because the scan of all the rows of a table is occasionally required, storing a table contiguously is a good idea. If the rows of the table were scattered and mingled with rows of other tables throughout the entire database, one disk record per row might have to be read to perform a table scan. If all the rows of the table are located together, then each physical disk record that is read brings in many rows from that table.

Note that many database systems offer the ability to change the ways rows are allocated to storage for performance (see Chapter 8).

Clearly, a database row must be allowed to be longer than a physical record on disk. This is easy to accommodate, by adding a pointer to each disk record that is the address of an overflow record in case a very long row must span to disk records. Alternatively, the row itself can contain a pointer to the storage block containing the continuation of the row.

5.5   Magnetic Disk Storage

Database systems make a collection of data available all the time by storing that data on disk storage devices that are always connected to the computer. Usually, the size of a stored database is too large for to be held in main memory. But even if there is enough main memory to hold an entire database, it is usually not desirable to tie up a large amount of main memory for a database that may not always be in use. Furthermore, main memory loses its content in a power failure; databases generally store information that must be reliably persistent and not lost if there's a power failure. Therefore, for all these reasons, relational databases are generally stored on magnetic storage devices.

Disk storage is very much slower than access to main memory, so the performance of any database operation is greatly affected by the number of disk data transfers needed to complete it. In fact, a database system typically performs many read/write operations and not much computing on the data that is transferred; therefore, the number of accesses, rather than what takes place in main memory, is the main factor in determining how long it takes to complete a database operation.

Because the database is stored on disk, many data structures that are designed for use in main memory are not applicable. Specialized data structures for use with disk drives have been developed that greatly improve database system performance.

5.6   Software Architecture

End-users access the database by using application programs that use the database system to interact with the database. The figure below illustrates this:

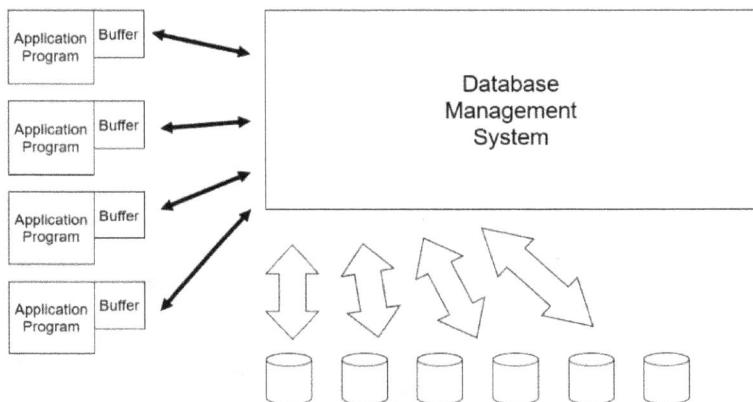

Figure 42. DBMS and Applications

Application programs interact with the database system by passing SQL statements to the database system and receiving status messages and results from the database system. The database system executes the operations requested by the SQL statements, keeps multiple applications from interfering with each other, and maintains the information necessary to recover the database in case of a software or hardware failure.

The database system reads and writes to the database; applications perform create, retrieve update and delete (CRUD) operations as the consequence of SQL statements that they submit to the database system.

5.7 Storage Architecture

Storage of the database is one of the principal drivers of many aspects of the design of the database system. Here the characteristics of the two principal storage devices are reviewed storage are reviewed, and then the methods used by database systems that provide good performance using disk are presented.

HDD

Figure 43. Disk Storage

A disk storage device is a rotating disk, called a platter, with a coating of magnetic storage material such as iron oxide. The platter rotates up to several hundred times a second, typically at 5,400, 7,200, 10,000 or 15,000 revolutions per minute. An arm that contains several read-write heads moves in and out, positioning the heads over tracks on disk where data is recorded.

A disk drive is accessed as a collection of fixed length records. To read or write one of these records, a program must wait for the disk to rotate so that the record is located underneath the read/write heads, called *rotational latency*. In addition, if the arm containing the read/write heads is not in the right position, there is an additional wait while the arm is repositioned, called *seek time*. Typically, it takes on the order of 10 milliseconds to access a disk record.

SSD

Recently, solid state drives (SSD) have dropped in price so that some HDDs may be replaced by SSDs, although they remain cost-prohibitive for very large databases.

An SSD contains multiple NAND flash memory components, from 10 to as many as 60 or 70, as well as some conventional dynamic random-access memory, DRAM, and a microcontroller. The microcontroller uses the DRAM to make the data storage in the NAND flash memories appear to be organized like an HDD.

Figure 44. SSD Storage Module[23]

Although SSD storage provides a dramatic performance enhancement over storage over an HDD, nevertheless it is still thousands of times slower than access to data in main memory, that is typically accessed in a few nanoseconds.

Thus, the workload of a database system consists of constant reading and writing, often waiting for that to take place, and a relatively small amount of processing.

Implementation

The database system doesn't perform its own reads and writes—those are done by the operating system—so the database system must use an operating system service for access to data. The

---

[23] Courtesy of StorageReview, https://www.storagereview.com/review/adata-s511-review-240gb.

stored database will have to appear to the operating system to be some standard file type that the operating system supports.

All modern operating systems have some form of a direct access file. That is, the operating system performs read and write operations on fixed length disk records, typically addressed by a record number starting with 1 in the file. The operating system is asked to establish a file of a certain number of records and allocates space to it. The operating system will then accept read and write requests by the relative record number within the file. The first record is number one, and so on to the last record. Database systems typically store the database in direct access files. This allows the database system to manage the content of the files without the operating system interjecting any overhead of its own. Because the contents of these files are typically swapped into and out of main memory, we'll call them database pages.

The only logical structure that a relational database system supports is tables, so what it stores on disk is rows. Rows are stored in pages on the disk, which of course are also sometimes in main memory. The database system will usually allocate areas of disk storage for each table, so that it can store all the rows of the table adjacent to one another, for speed in performing a scan of an entire table.

In addition to rows, the database system has one support structure that it uses, and that is indexes. So, there are some pages that do not contain rows; those are index pages.

5.8 Search Algorithms

All the CRUD operations that are performed by SQL statements either retrieve data, requiring data to be located before it can be retrieved, or they change data, requiring the data to be located before the change. Search is the first step in all database operations, so fast search is essential for good database performance.

Search algorithms for a database system must be tailored to the constraints of the HDD, which delivers fixed-size, large physical records after a considerable delay. Therefore, the index structures and search methods used for databases are different from those used in main memory, where any individual byte can be accessed quickly.

The B-tree and its search algorithms are so important that without the it, the relational approach might not be practical. Therefore, we discuss the B-tree in some detail, and its most important form, the B+ tree.

A useful adjunct to B-tree indexes is the hash index, that can provide extremely fast performance for a limited range of applications. Commercial database systems today often offer a hash index and a hash-based search in addition to the B-tree.

The discussion that follows starts with a review of search methods, assessing the applicability of each to data stored on disk, then concludes with B-trees and hashing.

Linear Search

The simplest approach to search is to the rows of the table in arrival order, and then, for search, start at the beginning of the table and examine each row. If the search is for a single unique value, then on the average if there are n rows, then approximately n/2 rows will be examined.

For a table of 1 million rows, this approach would require 500,000 accesses to the table. However, for a table of a few hundred rows, linear search would be practical.

Binary Search

For a binary search on the value of a single column, the rows must be stored in order by that column. The search starts at the midpoint, comparing the search value to the value at the midpoint. This comparison disqualifies either all the values higher than the midpoint value or all the values lower than the midpoint value. Then the second probe is at the midpoint of the rows that are still candidates. This continues, cutting in half the number of remaining candidates, until the sought value is located, or it is determined that the sought value is not present.

The diagram below illustrates a binary search of a series of ordered values from 1 to 15. Note that only the value of the column of interest is shown; for simplicity, the rest of the rows have been omitted. The search is for the value 15:

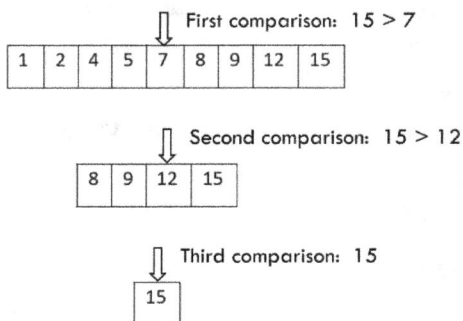

Figure 45. Binary Search for 15

The first probe is to the midpoint value, which is 7. Because the search value, 15, is greater than the midpoint value, 7, all the values below the midpoint are now disqualified from the search. The remaining candidates are the values 8 through 15. The next probe is the value 12, and the search value is greater than 12, so the next probe is to the only remaining value, 15, and the search value has been located.

Each probe of a binary search eliminates half the candidates; information theory tells us that each probe develops one bit of the address of the search value. Therefore, the average number of probes for binary search will be $\log_2 n$. This is a big improvement over linear search; for a table of 1 million rows, instead of 500,000 probes, for a binary search only 20 are needed.

However, binary search has its disadvantages. First, the rows must be kept in order; insertion of a new row near the beginning could require reorganization of the whole table. Also, since this is stored on disk, access to disk pages that are not adjacent could require extra revolutions of the disk.

Instead of storing the rows of a table in order to enable   binary search, an ordered index can be constructed with the values of one or more columns and the locations of the row associated with each value, so that binary search can be used with the index.   This permits binary search to be used on several different columns of a single table, through the creation of several indexes.

For simplicity of update, a linked structure can be used for the index.

Consider this example of a tree-structured binary search index for seven values. Again, only the search values are shown; in an index, the address of the row associated with each value would be included.

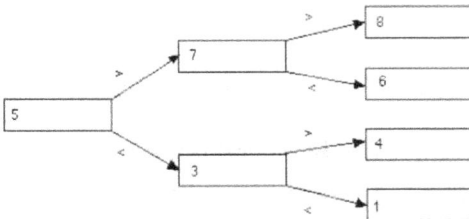

Figure 46. Binary Search Tree

Each node of this tree has just one value, and the pointers to the next note to be searched could lead off the page.   Allocation of these small nodes to disk pages so that the number of pages accessed during search is minimized would be very complex.

Another issue with binary search trees is balance. If the rows arrive in either ascending or descending order by the column being indexed, then all of them will be linked to the same side of the root, and the tree will essentially become a list, so that a search of this tree would be a linear search. The figure below shows a binary search tree that is perfectly out of balance, that would be constructed if the values arrived in descending order.

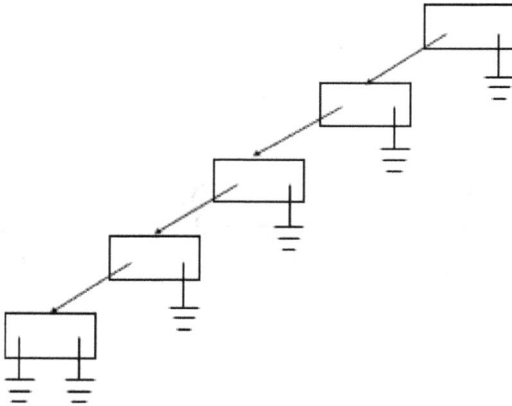

Figure 47. Out of Balance Binary Search Tree

A tree is said to be balanced if the lengths of all paths from the root to the leaves differ by no more than one. The tree of the figure above, in balance, looks like this:

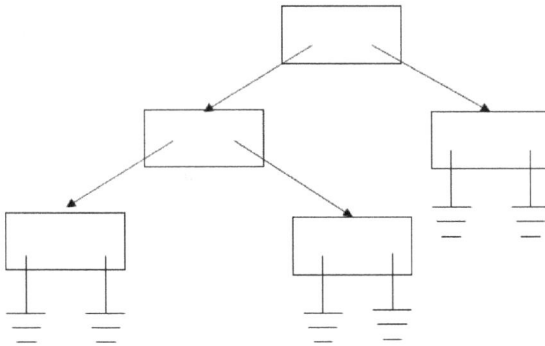

Figure 48. Balanced Binary Search Tree

What if, instead of storing just a single value at each node, we could store many values, so that single node of the search tree filled a disk page? Then the search tree would have a very high branching factor and would be very shallow, so it could be searched with a small number of accesses.

And what if there was a simple algorithm that would keep the tree in balance during insert and delete operations, so that the tree never had to be reorganized?

Such a tree structure exists, and relational database might not be practical without it. It's the b-tree, discussed in more detail later.

Hashing

Hashing is a search method with performance that is unmatched by any other approach. A hash function, that, given a column value x, will produce, as h(x), a value within a range of addresses is used. The hash function is applied to each column value of interest,

and then that value is stored in the index at that
address. These addresses might correspond to disk
pages, or to some multiple of disk pages.

The figure below illustrates the use of hashing for
search:

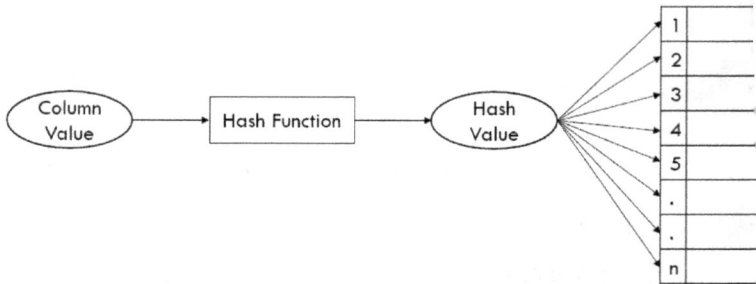

Figure 49. Hashed Search

To find a row containing a specific search value, the
hash function is applied to the search value, and that
address is checked to see whether it contains a row
with the column equal to the search value.

Note that the hash value always maps a larger range
of values (all the values of some column) into a
smaller range of values (the addresses used for
storage), so it is inevitable that some different
column values will map into identical addresses.
This is called a *collision*, and some provision must
be provided to deal with it. There are several
different approaches, that all involve some use of

additional space, connected to the principal address, often by a pointer.[24]

Using a well-designed collision-handling algorithm, it is possible for hashed search to locate a record of interest with an average of 1.2 accesses to the table. That is, collision-handling adds about 20% to number of accesses. Note, though, that the number of accesses needed is independent of the number of rows! So hashed access can locate any single row in a table of 1,000,000 or a billion or even a trillion rows in 1.2 probes!

However, hashing has one major disadvantage—it is limited to exact match search. Hashing does not preserve ordering, so hashing can't easily be used to process searches involving inequalities—such as finding all the people hired in February. That search would require a separate search for each day in February. Thus, while hashing is very fast for an exact match search, it cannot provide the foundation for relational database that is provided by the b-tree.

Implementation
There are two ways that the search algorithms described here can be implemented.

The first is to use these algorithms on the rows themselves. This method is used for small tables; the number of operations to open an index and process an index search is large enough that a linear search

---

[24] W.D. Maurer and T. G. Lewis, Hash table methods. Computing Surveys **7**, 1 (March 1975), 5 – 19.

will be as fast for a table on the order of several thousand rows. Of course, if no indexes exist, then the table itself must be searched, whatever its size.

For binary search or a hashed search, the rows would need to be organized according to the value of a single column in the case of binary search or the hashed value of a single column in the case of a hashed search. In both cases, the table would have its rows organized for search by only a single column, and that same search algorithm could not be applied to any other columns.

The second approach is to construct an index that supports the search and provides the address of the matching row once the sought value is found. This approach allows the table to be stored in arrival order, yet still be searched using either a hashed search or binary search for any desired column, provided the index has been established. The details of these indexes are discussed below.

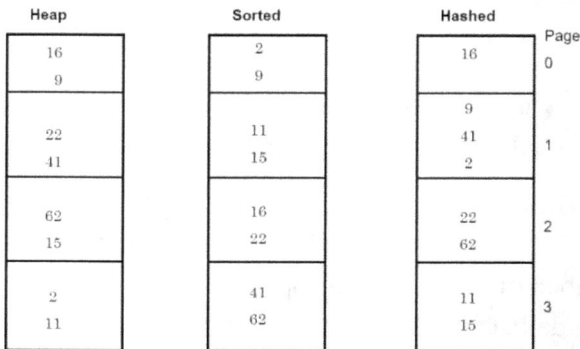

Heap	Sorted	Hashed	Page
16 9	2 9	16	0
22 41	11 15	9 41 2	1
62 15	16 22	22 62	2
2 11	41 62	11 15	3

Figure 50. Row Storage on Database Pages

Figure 50 shows three possible methods for storing rows on database pages. The first is what's called heap organization, where the rows are stored in the order they arrive, without respect to value. Such a storage arrangement allows for linear search. If the rows are stored in order by some column, then a search that takes advantage of ordering, such as the binary search, can be used. For hashed search, the rows would be stored in order by the hashed value of some column.

Clustering can also be used. With clustering, all the rows of several tables that share some common value in one of their columns are stored on the same database page. This is illustrated by Figure 51:

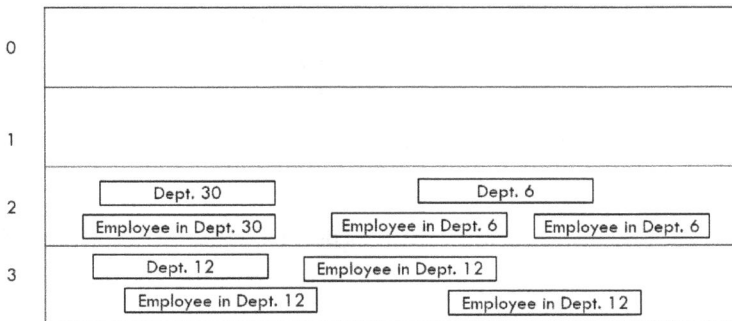

0	
1	
2	Dept. 30 Dept. 6 Employee in Dept. 30 Employee in Dept. 6 Employee in Dept. 6
3	Dept. 12 Employee in Dept. 12 Employee in Dept. 12 Employee in Dept. 12

Figure 51. Clustered Storage

In the figure, the rows of our example of employees and departments are clustered by the value of department number. Page two holds rows that have value 6 or 34 for department number, while page 3 stores rows that have department number 12. This arrangement offers the same performance advantage that would be obtained by de-normalizing and combining the department and employee tables.

Clustering illustrates an important advantage of the data independence that is offered by relational database systems. The performance of denormalized data can be obtained, along with the advantages of clarity and simplicity of programming of the normalized data model.

5.9 B-Tree Index

The first widely available paper about the b-tree index was published in 1972[25], although there had been internal publications at Boeing, where Beyer and McCreight were employed, as early as 1970, when the world was first learning about relational database management from Ted Codd's 1970 paper. Although the two technologies were not developed together, without the B-tree Index, relational database would not be as practical or widely accepted today.

The B-tree Index is designed to make efficient use of disk storage. The size of each node of the tree is increased to fill an entire page of HDD, so the branching factor of the tree gets very high. This makes the tree shallow, so that it can be searched with a small number of accesses. The problem of

---

[25] Bayer, R. and McCreight, E. M. Organization and maintenance of large ordered indexes. *Acta Informatica* 1, 3 (September 1972), pages 173-189.

balance is addressed by allowing the nodes of the tree to be only partially filled.

The B-tree diagrams here have been simplified. Each node of the tree has search values, that is, values for a single column for a table in the database and associated with each is the address on disk where that row can be found. For simplicity, all the addresses are omitted from these diagrams

When a B-tree is created, it has just one node, the root, that is created when the first value is entered. Suppose that first value is 1. The index would then have a single node, like this:

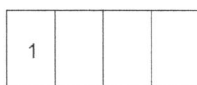

Figure 52. B-tree initial node

Now, if the values 4, 6 and 8 arrived, they would each be placed in that first node, so it would have this content:

Figure 53. B-tree indexing 4 nodes

Now suppose the next row in the table has value 5 for this column. We would like to put it between 4 and 6, but the node is full. When this occurs, we split the node into two, storing half the search values with lower values in the leftmost node and half the search values with higher values in the rightmost node, and we put the middle value in the node one level up in the tree. If there is no node one level up in the tree, then a new node is created at that level. After adding the value 5 to this index, it would look like this:

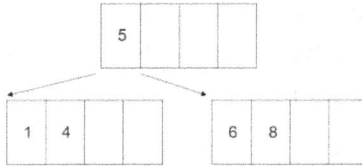

Figure 54. B-Tree with Value 5 Added

Note that this figure also shows pointers between the nodes. Each node of the tree needs to have space allocated for these internal pointers as well as the pointers to the rows containing the search values.

It's reasonable to ask how much space is sacrificed in the interest of balance. There have been some studies of how occupied the nodes of B-tree indexes are after a database has been in production for some time. Typically, index nodes are about 2/3 occupied.[26]

The B-tree, with all the content of each node included, looks like the diagram of Figure 55. In the diagram, each K is a search value, accompanied by a

---

[26] David M. Arnow and Aaron M. Tenenbaum, An empirical comparison of b-trees, compact b-trees and multiway trees. SIGMOD '84: Proceedings of the 1984 ACM SIGMOD international conference on Management of data (june 1984). Pages 33-46. https://doi.org/10.1145/602259.602265

pointer to the row containing that value. Then, associated with each value – pointer pair, there is a tree pointer to a lower node within the tree. That is the pointer that was introduced in Figure 12.

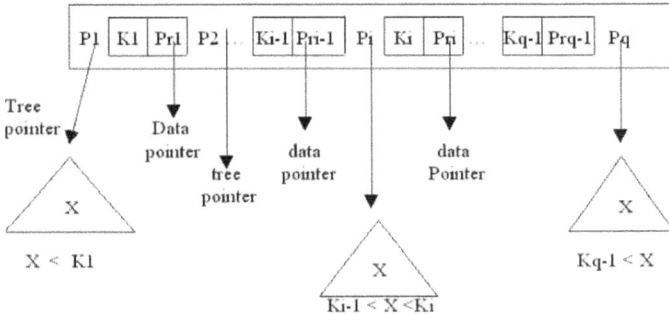

Figure 55. Full Content of B-Tree

in order to make full use of each page on disk, it's desirable for the node size of a B-tree Index to be the same as the page size. This can permit a large branching factor, which can allow the index to be very shallow, so that it can be searched in a small number of accesses.

B+ tree

The B+ tree is a refinement on the B-tree with important advantages for relational database systems. In a B+ tree, the leaves of the tree contain all the search values and their associated data pointers. In the nodes above the leaves, only enough search values are included to reach the proper page in the leaves, which is called the index set. This upper part of the tree, called the sequence set, has pointers only to other nodes in the tree, and no data pointers.

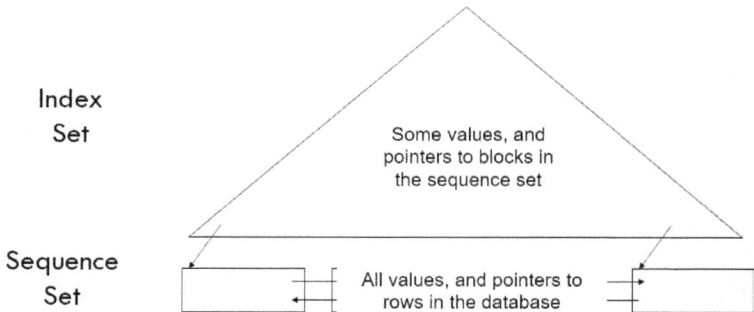

Figure 56. B+ Tree

Because storage addresses are not included in the index set, the branching factor of a B+ tree can be much greater than a B-tree. If data compression is applied to the search values in the index set, the branching factor can be increased even further. Depending on the length of the search values, and how effectively they are compressed, it can be possible to achieve a branching factor of 500 to 1,000 with the sequence set of a B+ tree.

Let's consider how many accesses a search requires if the branching factor is 500. Suppose the root of the B+ tree is fixed in memory, so that it can be searched without a disk access; thus, an index of 500 entries can be searched without any disk access. The table below shows the number of accesses required to search an index of more values. When the search of the index set is complete, one additional access to the sequence set is needed to obtain the disk address of the row that is sought.

Accesses	Rows
1	500
2	250,000
3	125,000,000
4	62,500,000,000

A search on an exact match in a table up to 250,000 rows can be carried out in 2 disk accesses! And a search for a single value in a table of any practical size can be completed in 4 accesses using a B+ tree.

The B+ tree offers another important advantage as well. The sequence set contains an ordered list of all the values in one column of the table that is indexes. To process a SELECT with an ORDER BY, the sequence set can be scanned to retrieve all the rows of the table in order by that column, eliminating the need to sort the results. For an inequality search, such as finding everyone who was hired in February, a search of the B+ tree for February 1 put us at the first value, and then we can scan along the sequence set to find the other values.

The B+ tree also enables merge joins to be carried out very quickly, reducing the number of operations from the product of the number of rows in the two tables being joined to the sum of the number of rows in the two tables. For tables of practical size, $m + n$ comparisons is a substantial saving over $m \times n$ comparisons!

Hash Index

The hash index is not fundamental to the operation of a relational database system, but it can offer huge performance advantages for the case that suits it best: a large table accessed by exact match. If a column is often used in inequality queries as well as for exact match queries, it's quite possible that a given column might be indexed by both a hash index and a b-tree index.

When hashing is used, the search value is processed by a hash function, that produces an address in the range of addresses in a hash table, when given a column value, as illustrated by the figure below:

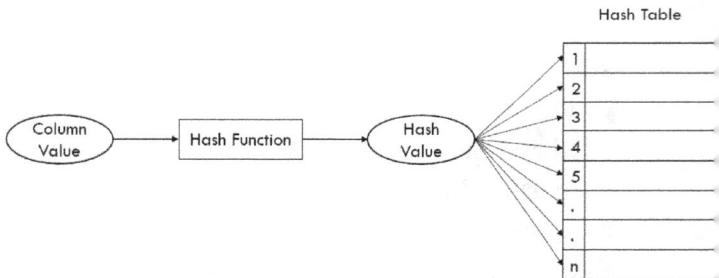

Figure 57. Hashing

If the rows are stored in a heap (see Figure 50, page 182), then this hash table can be stored on disk and used as an index.

Alternatively, the rows of the table could be stored on pages according to the hashed value of the column of interest, so that the hash value could be used to determine the page number of rows to be fetched, with their column value compared to the search value. This storage arrangement is called a hash cluster, and is illustrated by the figure below:

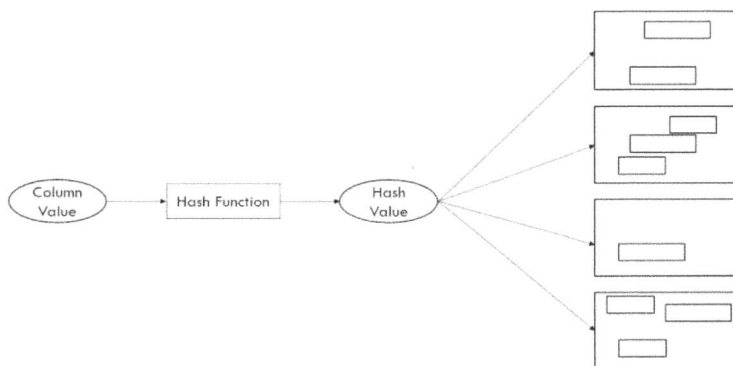

Figure 58. Hash Cluster

The hash cluster makes hashed access faster than the use of a hash index. However, if the table is searched based on the values of other columns, and is sometimes scanned, then storing it in a heap may be more efficient.

5.10   DBMS Software Architecture
Applications deal with the database system through shared buffers. The database system receives SQL statements from application programs. The database system then processes the SQL statement, accessing the stored database as needed, and returns results to applications. This is illustrated by the figure below:

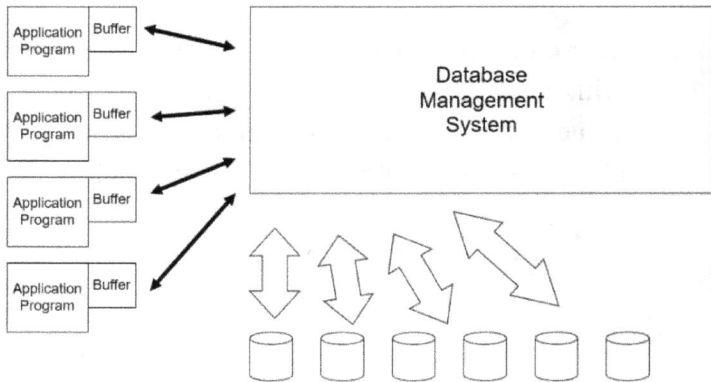

Figure 59. DBMS and Applications

The work area of the DBMS is memory that accessed by the DBMS and not applications that's used to serve all the applications, as shown below:

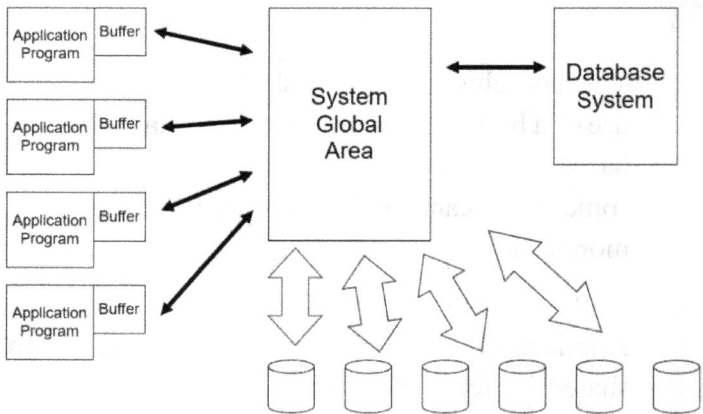

Figure 60. DBMS and Applications

The system global area (SGA) is used for interprocess information that is used by the DBMS. The paging area for database pages is within the SGA. When a page is changed, it is changed in memory and then a write operation for the page is given to the operating system. In addition, the lock lists that support locking of resources such as database pages and rows and index elements are also maintained in the SGA, as well as the list of active transactions that's written to the system log during checkpoint operations (see Section 7.6, page 243).

The database system logic that processes SQL statements has four principal components: the lexical analyzer, the SQL parser, the optimizer and the executor. These are shown in the figure below:

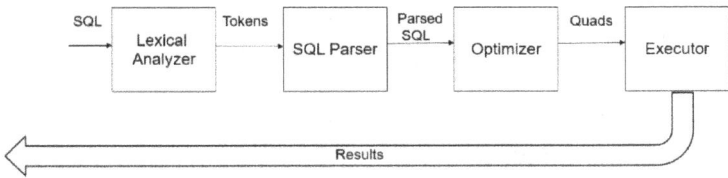

Figure 61. DBMS Software Components

The lexical analyzer receives a SQL statement from an application and analyzes the parts of the statement by category. For example, terms such as SELECT, FROM, WHERE are identified as reserved words. A column name would be identified as a column name. Operators would be identified.

Once lexical analysis is complete, then the SQL statement is analyzed by the SQL parser, which uses a grammar for SQL to identify the type of statement, check it for conformance to the grammar and to identify the operation that is requested. If syntax errors are detected, then the statement is sent back to application. Otherwise, the parsed statement, represented as a parse tree, is sent to the optimizer.

The optimizer (using the popular but technically incorrect name for it) has the job of selecting the strategy to be used to process the statement. This is performed by identifying various methods that can be used to process the statement, estimating the cost of each, and then choosing the lowest cost estimate. This process is discussed in Chapter 8.

Finally, represented by quadruples that each correspond to a basic operation of the database system, the action plan is passed to the executor, that carries out the plan, obtains the results, and passes the results back to the application.

The architecture for the executor is shown in the figure below:

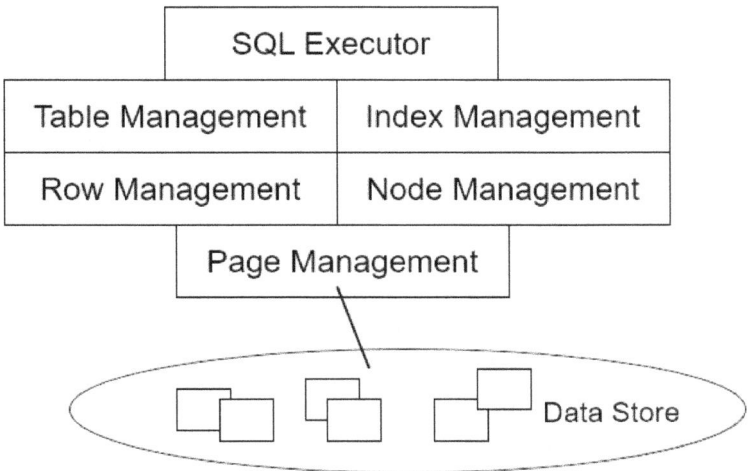

Figure 62. Executor Architecture

The executor has the job of carrying out the sequence of operations that have been selected for the SQL statement that's being processed.

The lowest level of the executor is the page manager, that receives CRUD requests for database pages. That is, it can create a new database page from an empty disk page, read a database page, update a database page or delete a database page. The page manager doesn't know or care about the contents of the page, simply manages pages.

The next level of the architecture is row management and node management. There are only two types of pages—those that contain rows and those that contain index nodes. Row management receives a request to fetch or change a row, then translates that to the relevant requests for pages and carries it out. Similarly, the node manager understands index nodes. It receives requests for accesses and updates for index notes and carries them out, issuing requests for pages to page management. Node management is where the algorithms that can split nodes when inserts are made and combine nodes when there are deletes.

Above row management is table management, that receives requests to act on tables, and carries them out in terms of rows by issuing commands to row management. At the same level, index management receives requests for index operations such as a search and carries it out by calling on index management.

5.11 Storage Architecture

A relational database is composed of tables, so storage for rows of tables must be provided. In addition, the database also has indexes, so storage for indexes is needed. Both kinds of structures are stored on database pages: table pages, that store rows, and index pages, that store nodes of indexes.

Today's database systems offer rich options regarding data types and how rows are stored. When you are writing a program, you'll want to review the offerings for your database system, with the needs for your application in mind. Here, to illustrate storage architecture, we discuss just one simple way of storing rows on disk.

For our example, consider a database system that offers just one data type—a variable number of characters. This can be used to represent a decimal number, or a character string.

It's necessary to choose a method for representing null values. For simplicity, for our example system, we'll represent null values in rows by missing values. That is, if a column has a null value within a given row, that column won't appear at all. A separate question, that impacts how a search for a null value can be conducted, is whether nulls are represented in indexes. Null can be represented by a missing value in a row, but represented explicitly in an index. Today's database systems have taken different approaches to this decision (see 00).

Having made these basic decisions, now we can decide how to store a row. Since all columns are variable length, we'll store a column length indicator, or <cli>, in front of each column value, or <cv>. Before the cli, we'll store the columnid, or <cid>. The cid can be assigned and stored in the table of columns in the system catalog at the time the table is created.

A row can now be represented by a sequence of triples of three values <cid>, <ci>, <cv>. And when there's a null value, we can just leave it out. A row will need two other pieces of information. It might not be necessary to identify the table, if rows are stored within a tablespace that contains rows of only one table. However, including a table identifier with

a row is good practice for testing the database code,
and for troubleshooting or even recovering a
database using a program that scans for rows that are
stored in the wrong location. Similarly, it's useful to
have a *rowid*, a unique number assigned to each row
as it's created. Note that the *rowid* is for internal use
by the DBMS and is not part of the data model.

Putting it all together, a row is represented like this:

<<tid>,<rid>,<cid><cli><cv>, ... , <cid>,<cli>,<cv>, ... >>

Figure 63. Row representation

When an index points to a row on a page, what's a
good structure for that index pointer? One approach
would be to use a page number and rowid as the
pointer, and then just scan the page to look for the
row matching that rowid. Of course, that consumes
CPU time in scanning pages. An alternative would
be to include on each page a small vector of pointers
to rows. Each would give the starting position of a
row. Then the index pointer could be a page number
plus an offset number to use in this vector, to pick up
the starting location of a row. That structure would
look like this:

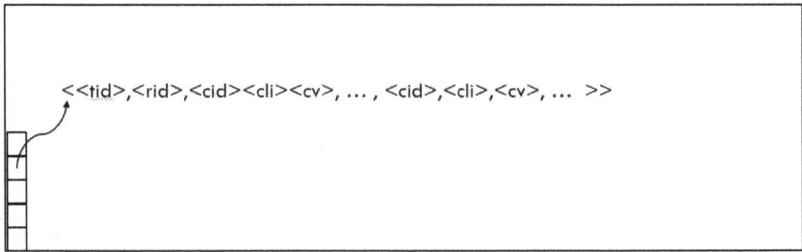

Figure 64. Row Storage on a Page

Extending the Database

Because the database is written and read by the operating system, it must be some file type that is known to the operating system so that it can tse the operating system's services for that file type. The file type that's generally used is a direct access file, that divides the file into equal-sized pages, and allows read and write access to them based on their relative address within the file.

When a database is created, the database system asks the operating system to create a file of a requested size, and that becomes the database. However, one file may not be enough for the database: data collections tend to grow, and, for performance, traffic to the database may need to be spread across more than one disk drive.

The notion of database extents allows a single database to be comprised of several operating system files. A database in general consists of some number of extents, where each extent is one operating system file. To add a new extent to a database, a CREATE EXTENT command is executed, that causes the database system to issue a request to create a file to the operating system. The database system treats this new extent as pages, giving them page addresses that start one greater than the highest page number in the previously allocated extent. The figure below shows how a database of three extents can be allocated across several disk storage devices.

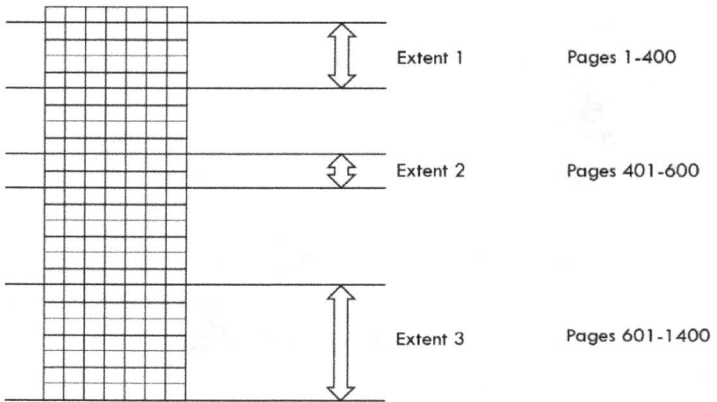

Extent 1   Pages 1-400

Extent 2   Pages 401-600

Extent 3   Pages 601-1400

Figure 65. Multiple Extents

System Catalog

A relational database consists of tables. Indexes are also used, to speed up access to data. There is a need for the database system to keep track of tables that are created, along with the location of tables within a database. For each table, it's necessary to record all its columns, along with data type, size, optionality and so on. It's also necessary to keep track of users who can access the database and the privileges they've been granted. Of course, it's necessary for the database system to keep track of all the extents, where they are located, their sizes, and so on.

The *system catalog* is used to keep track of all these, and other, created objects. The system catalog is a group of tables. When a new database is created, the database system creates the system catalog. Once the system catalog is created, then the database is ready to start creating tables, views, extents, users and other objects, and entering their characteristics into the system catalog.

For the database system that you're using, take some time to look at the system catalog. By looking at the contents of the tables in the system catalog, based on the ideas in this chapter, you'll be able to understand a lot about how the system works.

Chapter 6   On-Line Analytical Processing

6.1   Introduction

So far, this book has been concerned only with relational databases used for online transaction processing, or OLTP, allowing multiple concurrent processes to be changing values in the database at the same time, with high performance. This is an important use of relational database technology and forms the basis for the automated record-keeping and serving of online data for the largest organizations all over the world.

There's another important use of relational database technology: on-line analytical processing, or OLAP. OLAP is the use of the database to analyze historical data. For example, a study might be performed of salary trends in a company, compared with average salary data for the industry, obtained from an outside source. Data from the OLTP database is essential to this use, but there are some issues with the use of the OLTP database for analytics:

- OLAP use often involves joins of many tables, that can reduce OLTP performance, slowing down crucial on-line processes.
- Highly normalized data models are not efficient for analytical processing.
- Data from sources outside the organization, such as salary normative data or economic data, may need to be included in analysis.
- Data from years other than the current year may need to be included in analysis; OLTP

databases usually include only the current year's data.

- If the organization uses many databases, then data to be analyzed may be spread across multiple databases.

The figure below shows enterprise database use, with a single database management system but multiple databases. Note that there are transfer applications that run to move data back and forth between databases when information in one database is changed and must be copied into another database. This is a departure from the original promise of database systems, namely a single, integrated store of all the enterprise's data, free from duplication. This topic is explored further in Chapter 9.

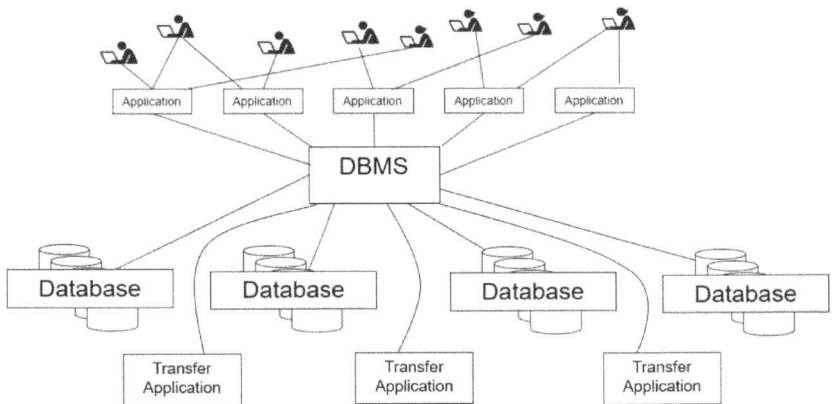

Figure 66. Multiple Databases

A separate store is generally used for data analysis, called the Data Warehouse, for all the reasons given above. It employs a data model that is especially suited to analysis, it often includes historical data that goes back beyond the current year, and it may also contain outside data that's used for comparative purposes. The figure below shows a data warehouse configuration. The database system vendors and others have developed products for extract, transform and load, or ETL, that are used to transfer data to the data warehouse.

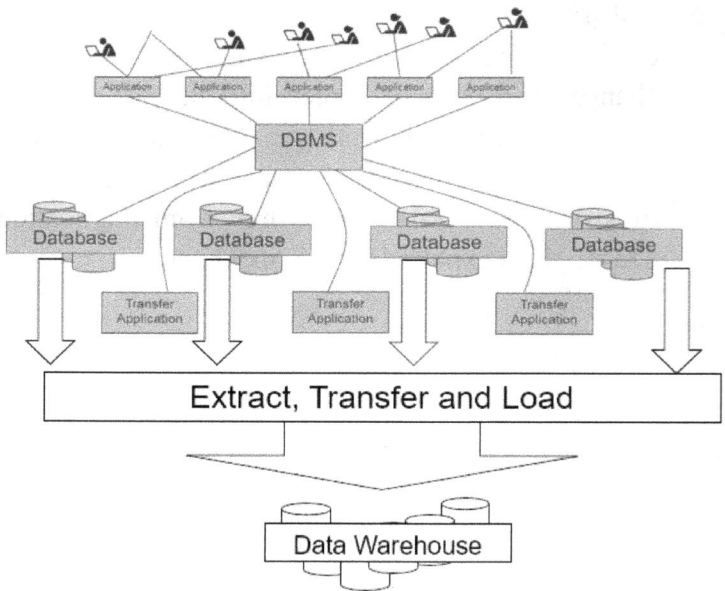

Figure 67. Data Warehouse

Because a data warehouse stores historical data, it can become very large. Therefore, while saving storage space is not generally an important goal when designing an OLTP data model, for the data warehouse, the situation can be just the opposite because of the potentially large number of entries. One of the principal reasons for using the star schema is its efficiency in use of storage capacity. The other important reason for using the star schema is that a special index, the bit map index, has been developed to improve the efficiency of the multi-table joins that are common for data analytics.

The star schema centers on some fact that is to be the basis for data analysis. For a retail store, for example, that fact is commonly the sale. Each row of the fact table in that case would characterize one sale. The categories for that sale would be stored in dimension tables, that would be connected to the fact table by a foreign key. The figure below shows a star schema.

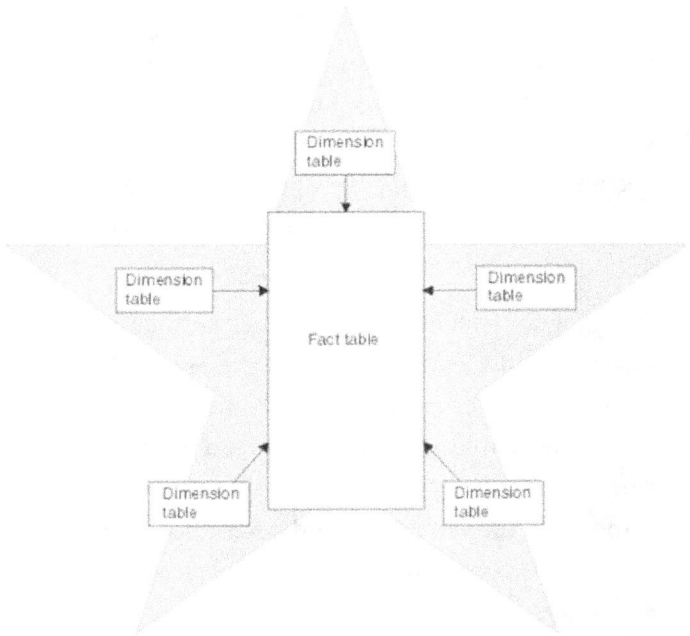

Figure 68. Star Schema

The star schema is also called a *dimensional data
model.* Each of the dimensions is an attribute of the
facts; the dimensions show bins of values. For
example, one dimension might be date. If date is
recorded to the day, in the fact table, then the
dimension table might have one row for each day of
each year covered by this star schema. The fact table
would have as its date attribute the primary key of
the date table. The attributes for a row could be the
day of the week, week of the year, month, year, day
of the year for that date. This data model allows
queries to be written in terms of any of the bins that
are established in the dimension tables, such as day
of the week.

Introduction   207

This figure shows an example of a star schema for a fact table of sales:

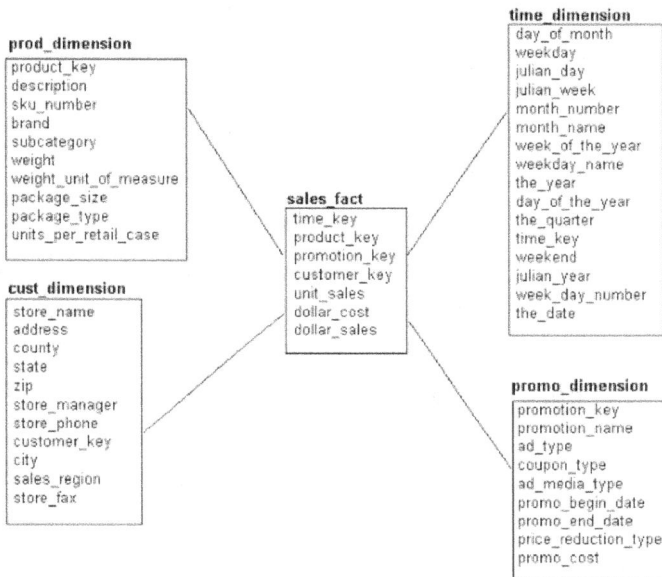

prod_dimension
- product_key
- description
- sku_number
- brand
- subcategory
- weight
- weight_unit_of_measure
- package_size
- package_type
- units_per_retail_case

cust_dimension
- store_name
- address
- county
- state
- zip
- store_manager
- store_phone
- customer_key
- city
- sales_region
- store_fax

sales_fact
- time_key
- product_key
- promotion_key
- customer_key
- unit_sales
- dollar_cost
- dollar_sales

time_dimension
- day_of_month
- weekday
- julian_day
- julian_week
- month_number
- month_name
- week_of_the_year
- weekday_name
- the_year
- day_of_the_year
- the_quarter
- time_key
- weekend
- julian_year
- week_day_number
- the_date

promo_dimension
- promotion_key
- promotion_name
- ad_type
- coupon_type
- ad_media_type
- promo_begin_date
- promo_end_date
- price_reduction_type
- promo_cost

Figure 69. Star Schema for Sales (source: Wikipedia)

A star schema does have limitations. First, it is purpose-built for analysis of the data in the fact table and is not suited for general-purpose OLTP use. In fact, it's not well suited for update at all; but, again, that's not its purpose. Second, it does not enforce data integrity well because of its denormalization. Loading data into a star schema data warehouse must be carried out with care to avoid creating anomalies that would automatically be prevented with the data integrity features of a normalized schema.

A variation on the star schema is the *snowflake schema,* which has multiple levels of dimension tables, with the outer dimension tables normalized. The snowflake schema, a special case of the star schema, is used to reduce total storage requirements. Dimension tables usually repeat values of dimensions many times, and the snowflake design reduces that duplication. The price paid for this savings in storage is the need to perform many more joins, reducing performance.

The figure below shows a snowflake schema for the star schema of Figure 69. The dimensions of the star schema have been "snowflaked" outward. For example, consider the Dim_Product dimension. The columns of Dim_Product have been snowflaked outward into lookup tables. In the star schema, Dim_Product included the full name of each brand; in the snowflake schema, Dim_Product includes only the Brand_Id, which is much smaller than the entire brand name. Each brand name is found only once in the Dim_Brand table.

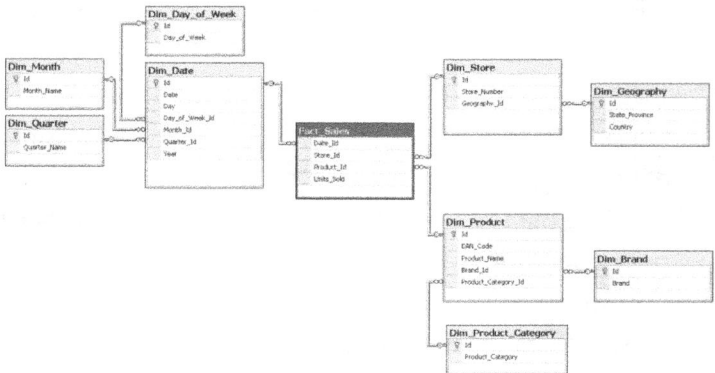

Figure 70. Snowflake Schema for Sales (source: Wikipedia)

Walmart has been a pioneer in the use of data analytics, and in the size of their data warehouse. Their data warehouse was the first one to reach size of one terabyte. The company now has more than 10,000 stores and serves more than 230 million customers each week in 25 countries. The company employs more than 2,000,000 employees worldwide, selling products from more than 25,000 different suppliers.

Walmart has been a leader in using their data warehouse to analyze sales patterns, to better understand how to interact with their customers, online and in stores. Neil Ashe, Walmart's CEO of global e-commerce said, in 2014, "We want to know what every product in the world is. We want to know who every person in the world is. And we want to have the ability to connect them together in a transaction."[27]

Information about every sale of every item at every Walmart in the world is transmitted to Walmart headquarters in Bentonville, Arkansas every day, so the business analysts working their can see trends up to the moment.

In one popular story of Walmart's use of the data warehouse, a store manager on the East Coast displayed a computer that was on sale prominently,

---

[27] Ashley Lutz, Insider, May 2, 2013. https://www.businessinsider.com/walmart-is-tracking-customers-2013-5

and sales for that store rose far above sales of other stores in the region. Enterprise data warehouse analysts saw this spike in sales, and Walmart corporate managers notified all store managers to display the computer in the same way, that highlighted the combination of a computer and printer for one low price. By the end of one day, sales in other stores had reached the level of the first store.

For many years, Walmart used star schemas for their data warehouse, but its size has grown beyond the ability of database systems. They now collect 2.5 petabytes of data from 1 million customers every hour. The company now uses big data technology for this task, a technology that supports analysis but does not offer transaction processing capabilities.

6.2   OLAP Products

The first data warehouse product was a hardware product sold as a complete data warehouse by Red Brick Warehouse, that ran a database system with a star schema database. The company had invented algorithms for rapid processing of joins involving star schemas, and sold the entire product as a closed box, keeping the algorithms private. An organization using the Red Brick problem would load their OLAP data into it, then use it as a data warehouse. The star schema optimizations in the Red Brick product delivered much higher performance for OLAP queries than could be obtained from other database systems.

Red Brick's approach to star schema query processing became known; it uses bitmap indexes. Sybase developed a stand-alone data warehouse product, separate from their database system, incorporating bitmap indexes for star schema processing. This product was not a general-purpose database system and was useful primarily for star schema processing. Oracle then developed a bitmap index product, by incorporating bitmap index processing into their relational database system. The same Oracle database system could now be used for OLTP and for OLAP.

IBM eventually purchased the Red Brick company, so now owns and offers a version of the Red Brick product. They also added the Red Brick optimization to their DB2 database system product. Sybase was acquired by SAP, who now offers their OLTP and OLAP products.

Many other OLAP products have been developed since those pioneering efforts, and the major commercial database systems now also offer OLAP features.

6.3   Processing Star Queries

Processing star queries relies on the use of bitmap indexes. The figure below shows a bitmap index on a table of employees, with department numbers from 10 to 40, and four job titles, Salesman, Manager, Janitor and Clerk.

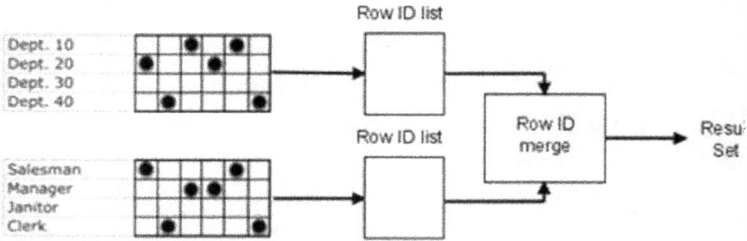

Figure 71. Bitmap indexes

The Figure shows indexes on the department number column and the job title column. The table has six rows; each index has one column for each row in the table. Each index has one row for every distinct value in the column. An OR operation can be performed by merging bitmaps corresponding to several values. This can be used to produce a list of row IDs that can then be merged with similar lists produced from other bitmaps.

A typical OLAP query is a join of foreign keys of dimension tables to the fact table. This is processed in two phases:

- The dimension tables are used to change the query so that it references the fact table, and bitmap indexes are used to retrieve the relevant rows from the fact table
- The result of this query is joined to the dimension tables, to retrieve the relevant bin names.

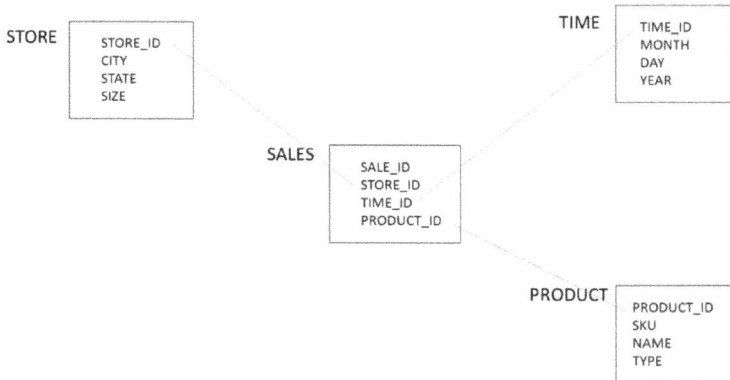

Figure 72. Example Star Schema

Consider the example above. Suppose the analyst wants to find sales and profits from the grocery departments of stores in the Web and Southwest districts over the last three quarters.

This is the query to find those results:

SELECT

    store.sales_district,

    time.fiscal_period,

    SUM(sales.dollar_sales) revenue,

    SUM(dollar_sales) - SUM(dollar_cost) income

FROM

    sales, store, time, product

WHERE

    sales.store_id = store.store_id AND

    sales.time_id = time.time_id AND

sales.product_id = product.product_id AND

time.fiscal_period IN ('3Q95', '4Q95', '1Q96') and

product.department = 'Grocery' AND

store.sales_district IN ('San Francisco', 'Los Angeles')

GROUP BY

store.sales_district, time.fiscal_period;

For phase 1, the query is modified to find the rows in the SALES table that satisfy the query, using bitmap indexes on the dimension tables:

SELECT ... FROM sales

WHERE

store_id IN (SELECT store_id FROM store WHERE

region IN ('WEST', 'SOUTHWEST')) AND

time_id IN (SELECT time_id FROM time WHERE

quarter IN ('3Q96', '4Q96', '1Q97')) AND

product_id IN (SELECT product_id FROM product WHERE

department = 'GROCERY');

Now the fact table is joined to the dimension tables. For dimension tables of small cardinality, a full-table scan of the table may be used; for large cardinality, a hash join may be used.

6.4   Data Modeling for OLAP

For OLAP, a star schema is an effective type of data model. Consider this OLTP data model for orders:

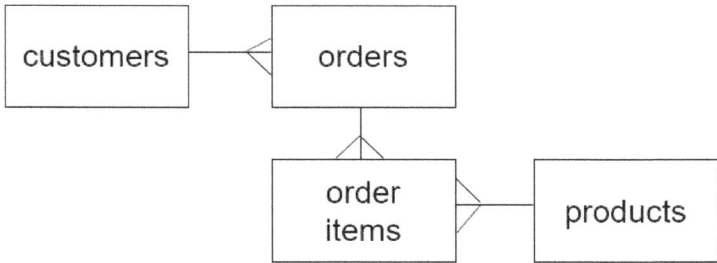

Figure 73. OLTP Data Model for Orders

To represent this information using a star schema, the orders table would be the fact table, and customers, products and time would become dimensions, like this:

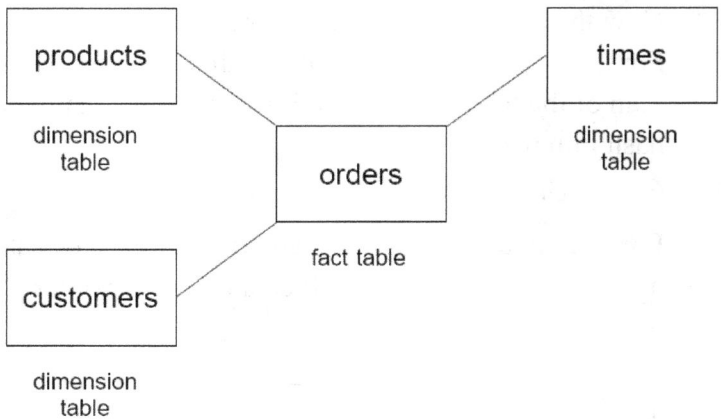

Figure 74. Star Schema for Orders

The Fact Table

The fact table contains the actual business process measurements or metrics for a specific event, called facts, usually numbers. Facts are represented in the fact table by foreign keys from dimension tables. These foreign keys are usually generated keys, to make them as compact as possible.

A data warehouse of monthly sales in dollars will have a fact table of monthly sales, one row per month. A data warehouse of retail sales will have a fact table that might have one row for each item sold.

Dimension Tables

Dimension tables have a small number of rows (compared to fact tables) but a large number of columns. For the lowest level of granularity in the fact table, a dimension table will have one row for each value, giving the category for each. A generated key is used to that the fact table reference to the dimension table can be small; the fact table tends to have a large number of entries and representing a fact by a four-byte integer (that can distinguish more than 4 billion values) is much more compact that spelling out the full text for the value.

This example shows the details of the star schema:

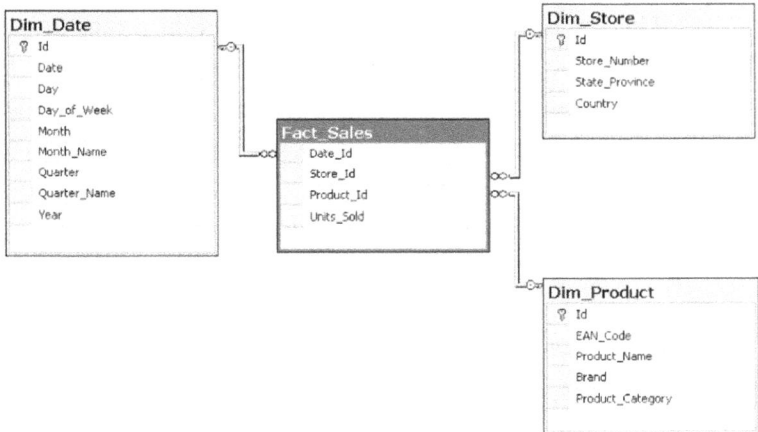

Figure 75. Star Schema Example

In the example, the attributes of the dimension tables show the "binning" of a single value from the fact table. The Date dimension table has a row for each date for a sale in the Sales fact table. For that date, the dimension table gives its date, the day, the day of the week, the month, the month name, and so on. This makes it possible for a query to be written looking for sales that take place on, for example, Tuesday. Phase one of query processing would convert "Tuesday" into its foreign key, and then phase two would use the foreign key to query the fact table and find all the sales that took place on Tuesdays.

The bins, or categories, in the dimension tables may be hierarchical or not; or some may form a hierarchy, and some may not. In the example above are some hierarchical categories and some that are not.

The level of granularity is known as the grain of the fact table. In the example above, the granularity is every sale of every product. The grain of the fact table determines its size as well as its ability to support fine-grained analysis. The finer the grain, the larger the table, and the greater its capability. A very large data warehouse may contain multiple star schemas at different levels of granularity, where some would be aggregations of the finest-grain schemas.

Design Approach

To design a star schema, the following four-step process can be followed:

1. Identify the Business Process: determine what business process the data warehouse represents. This process will be the source of the metrics.
2. Identify the grain: determine what one row of the fact table means. Is it monthly sales per location per product? Or is it every sale of every item in every store?
3. Identify the dimensions: the dimensions should be descriptive—that is, represented as

a character string—as much as possible, and conform to your grain.

4. Identify the facts: identify the specific metrics (or measurements, or facts). The facts should be numeric and should conform to the grain identified in step 2.

The Data Mart

Data mart is the term applied to a small-scale analytical database used by just part of an organization. For example, the finance department might have a data mart with just financial data, the personnel department might have a data mart of personnel data, and so on.

A department's data mart is typically run just for the needs of that department, and its star schema (or schemas) are intended for use only by that department. A data mart might be used in a department wishes to compare enterprise data with data obtained from other organizations, such as salary data, that they might be considered too sensitive to store in the enterprise data warehouse.

Data marts usually do not contain the lengthy historical information of a data warehouse; a data mart has only the historical information needed by a single department.

The nature of the queries run at a data mart may be very different from those at the enterprise data warehouse, and the subjects in a data mart may be only slightly related to the subjects in the data warehouse.

Chapter 7   Transaction Processing

7.1   Introduction

Transaction processing allows many processes to be performing CRUD operations on the database at the same time, with all of them reading and changing data, without interfering with each other, with each process producing the correct result.

The pioneer of transaction processing was Jim Gray of IBM, who was part of the original relational database research project at IBM Research. After leaving IBM, he went to Tandem, where he led the development of one of the first robust transaction processing systems. He wrote the definitive book on transaction processing, over 1,000 pages long.[28] Later in his career he joined Microsoft, who set up a laboratory for him in San Francisco.

Definition

A transaction is a unit of work, from the standpoint of a user of the system. This logical unit of work may involve a sequence of steps by the computer, but it is normally considered by the user as a single action. An example of a transaction would be an ATM action where a customer moved money from a savings account to a checking account. Within the database, the savings account balance needs to be

---

[28] Jim Gray and Andreas Reuter Andreas. *Transaction processing: concepts and techniques.* Morgan Kaufmann, 1993.

decreased and the checking balance increased, but to the user at the ATM, it's a single action. [29]

Jim Gray defined the ACID test for a transaction, that prescribes four conditions that a transaction must meet:

> Atomic: changes made by the transaction either all happen or none of them happen

> Consistent: at the start and end of the transaction the database is in a consistent state

> Isolated: the results produced by the transaction are the same as would be produced if nothing else was running

> Durable: once a transaction completes, the changes that it makes are permanent

For the example ATM transaction, consider what would happen if only part of the transaction was completed. If only the savings balance was decreased but the checking balance wasn't increased, then the customer would lose money, so the customer wouldn't accept this outcome. On the other hand, if the savings balance wasn't decreased but the checking balance was increased, then the customer would have gained, but the bank would lose money, so the bank wouldn't accept that outcome. The only

---

[29] Haerder, Theo and Reuter, Andreas. Principles of transaction-oriented database recovery. *Computing Surveys* 1, 4 (Dec. 1983), pages 287-317.

outcome acceptable to both parties would be to both decrease the savings balance and increase the checking balance, or to make neither change. Thus, the transaction is said to be atomic.

At the start of the ATM transaction, the database was correct—both the savings and checking balances for the customer were correct. However, if the savings balance was decreased first, then at that moment the database was inconsistent, because if all the customer's balances were added together, they would show an incorrect amount. When the transaction is completed by increasing the checking balance, then the database is once again in a consistent state.

The requirement for isolation allows for many processes to be performing CRUD operations on the database at the same time, without interfering with each other. For the ATM transaction example, it's necessary that the result of the transaction be the same, no matter what other transactions may be processed at the same time, perhaps at other ATMs.

The final requirement, durability, means that once the transaction completes, the changes it makes to the database are permanent. Certainly, this applies to the example of the ATM transaction—after moving money from savings to checking, it's necessary that the transfer be permanent, and the money does not return to the savings account.

Three SQL statements are used to perform transaction processing. BEGIN TRANSACTION indicates the beginning of a transaction. COMMIT WORK indicates the successful end of a transaction's processing; the database system makes the changes permanent, and ROLLBACK WORK is issued by an application when a transaction has failed.

The following discussion deals with a single database server with multiple processes accessing the database. Today, large IT complexes may delegate parts of a single transaction to multiple servers. However, all the techniques and principles described apply to multiple database servers accessing a single database and can be extended to a distributed configuration.

7.2   SQL Statements
Four SQL statements that are used to control transaction processing:

START TRANSACTION: begins a new transaction.

COMMIT WORK: indicates the end of a transaction's processing. Changes carried out by the transaction are made permanent.

ROLLBACK WORK: issued when a transaction cannot be completed. Removes any changes made by the transaction.

SET AUTOCOMMIT: disables or enables autocommit, which makes every statement atomic; that is, its changes are committed immediately.

An example of a transaction is the following:

> START TRANSACTION;
> UPDATE EMP SET SAL = SAL + 50
> WHERE EMPNO = 40;
> COMMIT;

7.3   Locking

The database system allows for multiple application programs to have access to the database and to be performing transactions all at the same time, preventing transactions from interfering with each other.

Locking is the method used to provide this concurrent read-write access to the database.

Three principal problems that are avoided using locking:

> Lost Update
> Uncommitted Dependency
> Inconsistent Analysis

Lost Update

Suppose two independent transactions, A and B, are underway, and X is a value stored in the database. Suppose this series of actions takes place:

1. A reads X
2. B reads X
3. A adds 10 to X
4. B adds 20 to X
5. A stores X
6. B stores X

Transaction A intended to add 10 to X, and transaction B intended to add 20 to X, so at the end of all this, the value of X should have increased by 30. But has it?

A and B read the same value. Then A increased the value of its version of X by 10, and B increased the value of its version of X by 20. Then A stores its value for X, which is overwritten by B's value for X. The value for X increases by only 20, instead of the increase of 30 that should have occurred.

A's update has been lost! Consider the impact if each of these changes was a deposit to an account. Now $30 has been deposited, say, by two people at different ATMs, but the value in the account has increased by only $20.

This problem can be avoided by permitting only one transaction at a time to be making changes to the same value.

Uncommitted Dependency
Again, suppose that two independent transactions, A and B, are running, X is a value stored in the database, and this sequence of actions takes place:

1. A adds 10 to X
2. B adds 10 to X
3. A performs a rollback

Now B's change has been removed because of the A's rollback. There is no net change to the value of X from these two transactions, when the value of X should have increased by 10.

The solution to this problem is to prevent B from making changes to X until after A has completed its work and commits the result. In other words, as in the lost update case, permitting only one transaction at a time to be making changes to the same value.

Inconsistent Analysis
Again, assume that A and B are independent transactions. R is a table with all values of $R_i = 20$. A is summing the values from R_1 to R_4, and B is reducing R_2 by 10 and increasing R_3 by 10. Suppose this sequence of actions takes place:

1. A reads R_1, sets sum=20
2. A reads R_2, sets sum=40
3. B changes R_3 to 30
4. A reads R_3, set sum=70
5. B changes R_2 to 10
6. A reads R_4, sets sum=90

A has calculated a sum of 90, but the sum before B's changes was 80, and so is the sum after B's changes. The changes being made by B while A was analyzing have caused an incorrect result for A.

The solution to the problem is to prevent any changes to any R value while A is calculating the sum.

Locking
Locking allows a transaction to reserve data that it is reading or changing, so that multiple transactions can run at once, all making changes to the database, without interfering with each other.

228 Chapter 7 Transaction Processing

The major correctness criterion for execution of concurrent transactions is *serializability*. A schedule for executing transactions is said to be serializable if its results are the same as the results of running the transactions serially—that is, one after the other. Serializability is not concerned with which transactions run first, only that the result does not reflect any mixing of the results of the transactions.

Locking is used to serialize transaction execution schedules.

Two types of locks are used:

- Read (also called shared): allows other transactions to hold read locks on the same data, and to read the data
- Write (also called exclusive): permits no other locks to be held on the same data until it is released, and permits no operations on the data except by the lock holder

In the examples above, if the transaction that was summing elements of R obtained a read lock on R before starting, then B would not be permitted to make changes in R while A was calculating its sum, and A would have produced the correct result. This would prevent the occurrence of the inconsistent analysis problem.

The lost update problem can also be solved with locking. If transaction A had locked X upon reading it, then A could have made it changes to X, then released its lock. B would be prevented from reading

X until A had made its changes, so B would start with A's changes, so the result would be correct.

Finally, the uncommitted dependency problem can also be solved by locking. If transaction A held a lock on X until it changed its value, then B would start with A's changes already final, and B's rollback would leave A's changes in place.

Use of Locks
There are simple rules for the use of locks by transactions:

- Before reading, acquire a read lock on all the data to be read, and hold the lock until all needed values have been read, then release it.
- Before updating, acquire a write lock on the values to be changed, hold that lock until the transaction completes, then release it.

SQL normally operates in the AUTOCOMMIT mode, so that locks are acquired on all values to be changed by an UPDATE statement, then released after the changes have been made. AUTOCOMMIT can be turned off for transaction processing with the statement SET AUTOCOMMIT OFF.

For transaction processing, SELECT FOR UPDATE acquires exclusive locks on all the values that are read. The lock is released when a COMMIT or ROLLBACK statement ends the transaction.

If a lock is requested for values that are already locked, then the rules laid out in the lock compatibility matrix determine the disposition of the request.

Lock Type	Read-Lock	Write-Lock
Read-Lock		x
Write-Lock	x	x

Figure 76. Lock Compatibility Matrix

The first column shows the initial lock held; the two following columns show the action when a second lock is requested by another transaction. The first row tells us that if a read lock is held and another is requested, it is granted. Any number of transactions can hold a read lock on a single item. However, if a read lock is held and a write lock is requested, it is denied.

The second row tells us that if a write lock is held, then no others locks of any type are granted until the transaction concludes and gives up its write lock.

The diagram below illustrates the logic of lock processing:

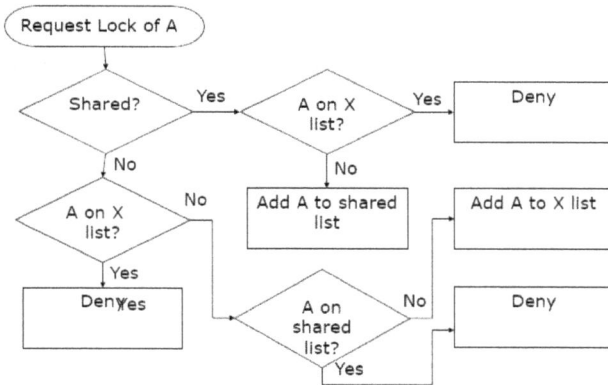

Figure 77. Lock Processing

Lock Implementation

Locks are implemented within the database as lists of the items that are locked. That is, there is a list of read locks, that shows the transaction identifier and the identifier of the data that is held for each read lock. Similarly, there is a list of write locks, with similar information about every write lock.

When a transaction requests a read lock, the lock manager checks the list of write locks, and denies the request if there is a current write lock on that data; the requesting transaction then waits for the lock to be granted. Once the lock is granted, it is added to the list of read locks. If a write lock is requested, both lists must be checked, and the lock denied if there is an existing read or write lock. If there is no lock, then the write lock is granted and added to the list.

If there are many concurrent transactions, lock lists can become long. Since lock lists are scanned every time a transaction starts, lock list searches can become one of the main performance bottlenecks of the database system. For this reason, sophisticated structures are used for structuring lock lists so that locks can be located rapidly.[30]

Lock Granularity

Locking can be performed at different levels of granularity. For example, consider an example of coarse granularity, namely locking at the table level. That is, if a transaction was to change any values in the table, the whole table would be locked.

At this level of granularity, the number of locks could never exceed the number of tables in the database, so the lock lists would be short, and little CPU time would be consumed in scanning the lock lists. In addition, at this level of granularity, the amount of information needed to identify the resources locked would be just table names, so the elements of the lock lists would be short. Of course, this would put sharp limits on the number of concurrent processes that could operate.

Consider the opposite level of locking granularity, an individual column value in a row. Now the lock list must contain a table identifier and a row identifier and a column identifier. In addition, at this fine level

---

[30] Kimura, Hideaki, Graef, Goetz and Kuno, Harumi. Efficient locking techniques for databases on modern hardware. Third International Workshop on Accelerating Databa Management Systems using Modern Processor and Storage Architectures (ADMS '12), 2012.

of granularity, the lock list is likely to be quite long. However, with fine granularity, transactions are less likely to interfere with each other, so greater concurrency will be possible than with coarse locking.

Clearly, finer granularity permits greater concurrency of operation, at greater cost of lock management.[31] There is a consensus around row-level locking. This choice permits significant concurrency, at the expense of potentially lengthy lock lists. Database systems using row-level locking have more elaborate design of their lock lists so that they don't become a performance bottleneck.

7.4   Deadlock

At this point, having considered the types of conflicts that can occur from concurrent access to the database by many processes, it's tempting to think that all the problems of concurrency have been solved. Unfortunately, that's not the case—another serious problem is known, that must also be dealt with. This explanation of deadlock is the famous hypothetical story of the Four Philosophers, from Prof. Edsger W. Dijstra, a renowned Dutch computer scientist, who made many crucial contributions to our field.

In Prof. Dijstra's story, a new philosophy department is being formed in the university. The desire is for the department to be as efficient as possible, so all

---

[31] Ries, Daniel and Stonebraker, Michael. Locking granularity revisited. *ACM Transactions on Database Systems*, Vol. 4, No. 2 (June 1979), pages 210-227.

the procedures are designed from the outset for productivity. For a philosophy department, that means lots of papers; and if the philosophers are to write lots of papers, then plenty of time must be available for thinking, with few interruptions. There will be just four philosophers.

The offices are set up without telephones, to avoid interrupting any thinking. So that lunch won't be a big distraction from the day's work, a lunchroom is provided for the department, with special rules. Since conversation would be a distraction, the meal must be eaten in silence, with all talking forbidden. The lunchroom is laid out with four places at the table, and four chairs, like this:

Figure 78. Philosophy Department Lunchroom

There is always a bowl of fresh spaghetti, with sauce, in a serving bowl in the center of the table. Around the table are four plates, one for each professor, and four forks.

Lunch, like the rest of the day, takes place according to strict Department rules. Each philosopher can eat lunch at any time. When eating lunch, the philosopher enters the lunchroom and sits at an empty chair. Because there are four chairs, there will always be an empty chair. Then the philosopher turns to the right and picks up a fork and turns to the left and picks up a fork, then uses the two forks to take serving of spaghetti. After this, the fork on the left is put down, and the philosopher eats, using the fork on the right. Since one or both forks may already be in use, when this happens, the philosopher waits, in silence, until the needed fork is put down, then proceeds to eat, according to department rules.

The four philosophers are hired, and the department begins operation. Because the philosophers have a lot of time for thinking, many quality papers are written and accepted by important publications, bringing accolades to the department and the university.

Then, one day, by purest coincidence, all four philosophers decide, each on their own, to have lunch at just the same time. They all enter, and they each take a chair at the same time. Then, following the rules, each reaches to the right and picks up a fork, so that each holds the fork that used to sit at the right.

Then each philosopher turns to the left and sees no fork. That's no problem, because the department rules provide for this situation: simply wait in silence for the fork to be put down.

The four philosophers now each must wait for the left-hand fork to be put down, but it won't be put down, because the philosopher to the left is also waiting for the fork on the left and can't start eating.

Since the philosophers aren't allowed to talk to each other, this continues until the philosophers starve, ending the short but successful existence of the philosophy department.

From a transaction processing point of view, we can say that there were four transactions, each waiting on a resource held by another transaction. In this whole chain of four transactions, none could complete. This is called *deadlock* or *deadly embrace.* Whenever a transaction that can't get all the needed resources hangs onto the resources that it does have, then deadlock can occur.

For the philosophy department, the solution is simple: change the fork rule so that if the left fork is not available when the philosopher tries to pick it up, then the philosopher puts down the right fork and starts the process over.

Requiring a task to request all its resources in advance, and then take all of them or none of them, is an approach that enables operating systems to avoid deadlock. This approach would have each philosopher pick up either both forks or no forks.

However, that approach won't work for database systems, because at the start of a transaction, not all the resources needed for the transaction may be known. Which values will be changed may depend on data to be read during the transaction.

For database systems, it's necessary to detect deadlocks, then roll back one of the deadlocked transactions and restart it.

An early method used to detect deadlocks was elapsed time, which was used by Tandem. If a transaction didn't complete within a specific time interval, it was judged to be deadlocked, and was rolled back and restarted. Since deadlocked transactions do not complete, this method will eventually detect all deadlocked transactions. However, transactions that deadlock long before the time interval expires will continue to hold locks, potentially causing other deadlocks, until the interval completes. In addition, there will false positives— particularly when the system is very busy, transactions that are operating properly may take longer than usual to complete and will be rolled back unnecessarily.

The Waits-For Graph
An algorithm has been developed that provably detects all deadlocks as they occur, so that only transactions that are deadlocked are rolled back.

A directed graph called a *waits-for graph* is used. Each node represents a transaction, and each arc shows that one transaction waits for another. Figure

79 shows a waits-for graph of five transactions. T1 waits on T2, T3 and T4 to release locks before it can proceed. Each other transaction waits on only one transaction.

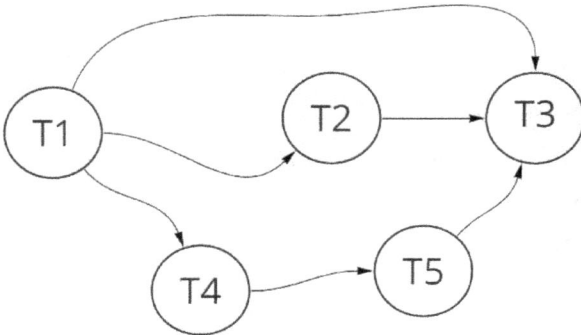

Figure 79. Waits-for Graph.

Every time a transaction requests a lock and must wait for it, the graph is checked. If the wait is not already represented on the diagram, then it is added. When all the locks that a transaction waits for from another transaction are granted, then an arc is removed from the graph.

The graph is regularly checked for loops; a loop indicates that a deadlock has occurred, and a transaction must be rolled back. Usually a "junior" transaction is rolled back; by one of several measures. The transaction to be rolled back might be the one with the shortest elapsed time since starting, or the transaction holding the fewest locks.

The graph doesn't have to be checked after every update; after all, if there's a deadlock, it will still be there a few database operations later.

Livelock
There is another effect that can take place in a transaction processing environment that produces results like deadlock, called *livelock.*

Consider a priority scheme that gives high priority to new requests, so that short new requests are serviced quickly, and won't wait for resources behind longer-running requests. This approach is appealing because it gives quick service to requests that complete quickly.

The first use of this approach was for time-sharing systems, where long-running programs tended to slow down service for everyone. If new program executions got priority, then long-running applications would get lower priority, which was desirable. Unfortunately, the long-running programs would not get much cpu time and would run—and take up memory—for very long periods. The system would become clogged with long-running problems that received so little cpu time that they might never complete.

The same difficulty can occur with transaction processing in a relational database system. Happily, the problem is easily avoided, by not assigning higher priority to new transactions.

7.5   Transaction Scheduling

The waits-for graph provides a reliable method for detecting deadlocks so that a transaction can be rolled back. However, rollbacks are undesirable: the rollback itself consumes resources, as well as wasting whatever resources the transaction used before rollback. Transaction scheduling algorithms are used to reduce the number of deadlocks that occur.

If transactions can run in any order, and begin acquiring locks, deadlocks will occur. Consider this scenario for transactions A and B:

Transaction A	Transaction B
Requests lock on x	Requests lock on y
Locks x	Locks y
Requests lock on y	Requests lock on x
Waits for lock on y	Waits for lock on x

After these operations, transaction A has a lock on x and waits for B to release its lock on x, while B waits for A to release its lock on y.   A deadlock has occurred! One of these transactions must be rolled back and restarted while the other one completes.

It's also necessary to consider when locks are placed and released by a transaction.   Consider this sequence of operations:

T1 read locks x, reads x, updates x

T2 write locks x, writes x, write locks y, writes y, unlocks x and y, commits

T1 write locks y, writes y, write unlocks y, commits

In this case, the change that T2 has made to y will be lost.   If T1 had held its read lock on x until it committed, then this error would not have occurred. Note that this is a form of the lost update problem discussed on page 225.

Choices can be made regarding which transactions are permitted to start, even before a lock is requested, that can reduce the number of deadlocks that will be produced: this is the job of the *transaction scheduler*.

The simplest transaction schedule is to allow only one transaction to run at a time; this avoids all deadlocks, although at great cost in concurrency. Another approach would be to require a transaction to request all the data it needs to lock at the start of the transaction, so that its lock requests could be granted all at once.   Unfortunately, this won't work for a database system, since a transaction may not know what changes it will make until transaction processing is underway.

At   the   opposite   extreme,   simply   allowing transactions to proceed without any supervision at all would result in many deadlocks.

Two-Phase Locking
Two-phase locking is a protocol that reduces the number of deadlocks:

1. Expanding phase: locks are acquired, no locks are released
2. Shrinking phase: locks are released, and no new locks are acquired

There are more restricted levels of two-phase locking protocols, that each prevent additional deadlocks. Consider this example:

Strict Two-Phase Locking
With *strict two-phase locking*, the transaction complies with two-phase locking; in addition, it releases its exclusive locks only after it has ended by either committing or rolling back. Shared locks can be released during phase 2.

Strong Strict Two-Phase Locking
Strong strict two-phase locking, a further refinement, requires that both exclusive and shared locks acquired by a transaction are released only after the transaction has ended. A transaction that follows this protocol has a phase 1 that lasts for the entire transaction, and a degenerate phase 2.

The protocol most frequently used in today's database systems is strong strict two-phase locking.

Distributed Transactions
We have assumed up to this point that there is a single database server that maintains a single lock list and waits-for graph. It may be necessary for a transaction to make changes in several independent databases that don't have a common server. A method to synchronize a transaction across independent database servers is needed, so that locks can be placed to avoid errors, and errors and deadlock can be avoided, even if some of the resources that are locked by a single transaction are

in different databases, with different database servers.

A protocol called two-phase commit is used in this case.

In the first phase, each server is sent its part of the transaction, along with the command PREPARE TO COMMIT. This causes the server to obtain the needed locks, process its part of the transaction, but not commit. Each server reports back READY TO COMMIT to the initiating server.

In the second phase, if any server can't complete its part of the transaction or does not report success within a reasonable time interval, then all receive a ROLLBACK command. Once all servers indicate that they are ready to commit, then the COMMIT command is issued to all servers, and they commit their changes.

7.6   Recovery

Recovery from failure is essential for a database system. The data stored in a database can be so important to an enterprise that it might not be able to survive its loss. Imagine a bank the size of Citibank, with a database storing all of Citibank's account information for all its customers. If this database is lost, the ability to account for billions of dollars would be lost. If the database is damaged, it must be restored to its state just before the failure.

Recovery is not just a desirable feature; for a transaction-processing database system, recovery is essential.

There are two causes of loss of a database: loss of media, such as a failure of a hard drive, and a software failure, where the media is not damaged.

Backup copies of the entire database are made regularly and are stored in a location away from the computer, so that even the destruction of the computer room won't cause loss of the database. Recovery from a media failure involves copying the most recent backup copy into the database, then running a recovery program to restore all transactions that were processed since the backup was made. When a software failure occurs, and there is no media damage, the same recovery process is used, but without restoring the database from a backup. A log of transactions produced by the database system is used to bring the database up to date.

Recovery is complicated by the delay between the time the database commits a transaction and the time it is written to disk, when the data is held in operating system buffers, waiting on the disk drive to process the writes. It's possible for a transaction to be committed by the database system but not written into the database if a failure occurs after the commit but before the write.

The database system keeps a log of every change to the database made by every transaction, with the value of data before and after the change, called the *before image* and *after image*. If a transaction makes changes at different times, it may produce multiple log records.

WAL, or write-ahead logging, is used by all database systems. Before a change is written to the database, the log entries must be written. Usually, positive interlocks are used to assure that WAL is followed. To ensure that a copy of the log is available for restoration, two independent copies of the log may be written.

Whenever the database is changed, the LSN of the transaction making the change is written on the database page that's changed. Thus, every database page shows the LSN of the last transaction that changed a value on that page.

In addition to the before and after images of transaction changes, and entries that show when a transaction has committed, the log also contains checkpoint records, made every time a checkpoint is taken. During a checkpoint, all the operating system buffers are emptied, so that all pending writes are complete. Then a checkpoint record is produced that shows all active transactions at that time.

When a recovery is performed, first the database is restored to the time of failure, if it has been damaged. Then the log is used to apply changes from the log to the database that have not already been applied.

The recovery process must assure that transactions that were in process at the time of the failure are completed, if there is enough information to complete them, or completely removed.

There are two actions that are employed in the recover process:

1. Redo—repeat all changes made by a transaction, ensuring that every change the transaction originally made has been completed. Changes that were made correctly are not repeated.

2. Undo—reverse all the changes made by a transaction, restoring the database to its state before the transaction started.

Recovery uses the most recent checkpoint record in the log to guide the process. Reading the log forward from the checkpoint record, redo is applied to every transaction shown in the log, until the end of the log is reached. At this point, the recovery process goes backward, and applies undo to every transaction that doesn't have a commit shown in the log.

The effect of this process can be seen in this figure, that shows five transactions, T1 through T5, that had started and committed at different times.

T1 started and committed before the checkpoint. Since all the buffers were flushed at the checkpoint, all the changes for T1 have been written to the database, and no recovery action is needed. In fact, the recovery process will not even see T1.

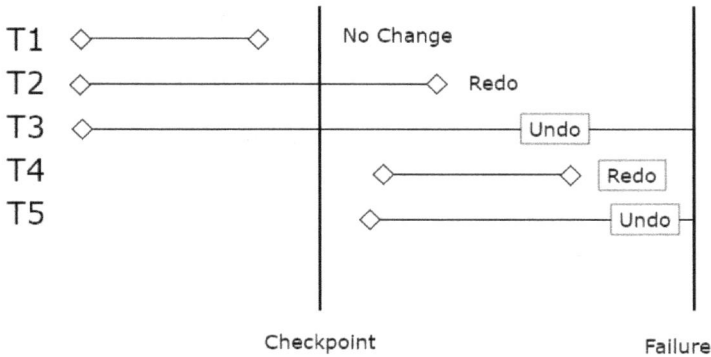

T1 ◇————————◇ No Change
T2 ◇——————————————◇ Redo
T3 ◇———————————————| Undo |
T4 ◇——————————◇ | Redo |
T5 ◇————————————————| Undo |

Checkpoint   Failure

Figure 80. Log Analysis

T2 started before the checkpoint and committed after the checkpoint. Thus, T2's changes, although they are all known and shown in the log, may not have been written to the database, since T2 continued processing after the checkpoint. T2 receives the redo action.

T3 started before the checkpoint but had not committed at the time of the failure. Therefore, the log may not show all the changes that T3 would have made, so T3 can't be redone; it must be given the undo action to back out all the changes that it made.

T4 started after the checkpoint and committed before the failure, so all its changes are in the log, although they may not have been written to the database. T4 receives the redo action.

T5 started after the checkpoint but had not committed by the time of failure, so T5 might have made other changes if it had run to completion, so T5 receives the undo action.

This recovery method has some disadvantages. Each checkpoint requires that acceptance of new transactions must be stopped while the buffers are flushed. If this happens in the middle of a busy day, when customers are using point of sale terminals for purchasing or are using ATMs, such a pause is unwelcome.

Fortunately, there is an advanced algorithm for recovery that gives the same result, without the need for suspending transaction processing for checkpoints. This algorithm, invented by IBM (surprise!), was published in a landmark paper in the ACM Transactions on Database. Systems in 1992[32] and has subsequently been widely adopted.

ARIES uses write-ahead logging to ensure that the log is always written before database changes are made. It also introduces the log sequence number, LSN. Every log record is assigned an LSN in ascending order. Although the LSN does not directly represent time, it is effectively a time stamp, because a log record with a greater LSN must have been produced by a transaction that was processed later. When any database change is made, the LSN assigned to the log record is also written on the database page that is changed. Thus, it's possible to

---

[32] C. Mohan, D. Haderle, B. Lindsay, H. Pirahesh, P. Scharz. *ARIES: A transaction recovery method supporting fine-granularity locking and partial rollbacks using write-ahead logging.* **ACM Transaction on Database systems, 17,** 1 (March 1992).

discern which of the changes in the log have been written into the database. If a database page has an LSN of X, then every change to that page shown in the log that has an LSN less than X has been written.

When a checkpoint is made, ARIES does not require the buffers to be flushed. Instead, the checkpoint record includes a list of all transactions and their states, the LSN of the most recently written log record for each transaction, and any unwritten changed data that is in the buffer pool.

The ARIES log analysis starts from the most recent checkpoint record. It goes forward, to the end of the log, bringing its information about transactions and dirty pages (that is, pages with incomplete changes) up to date. Then, in the redo pass, ARIES makes all updates that were not written to the database, for all transactions. In the redo process, the update shown in a log record is repeated if the database page's LSN is less than the log record's LSN. After the redo pass, the database is in the state just before the failure. The undo pass now starts at the end of the log, rolling back all transactions that did not commit before the failure.

These are just the highlights of the ARIES algorithm, omitting important features such as how it handles a failure that occurs during recovery. The original paper has a complete description of all aspects of the algorithm and is recommended as a good survey of all the ingredients of database recovery.

.

Chapter 8   Query Processing, Performance

8.1   Introduction

Prior to the introduction of the relational approach, all the logic of retrieving data from the database was built into applications, so solving a performance problem usually required changes to the application.

With the relational approach, things have changed. The application program passes a SQL statement to the database system; the SQL statement defines what is to be retrieved, but not how to obtain it. The database system is responsible for choosing an efficient strategy for the retrieval. Thus, if an adjustment is made to the physical structure of the database to improve performance, the application doesn't need to change.

Given that the database system chooses the processing strategy, and the application program has no control over this process, what does an application programmer do if there's a performance problem?

This is where some knowledge of how the database system works is helpful. Compare this to driving a car. You can drive a car for a long time without understanding how any of the car works, based just on understanding the user interface of the pedals, steering wheel and so on. But when the car isn't running properly, knowing something about how the car works will help you make a good decision about how to handle the problem.

Similarly, when a SQL statement is running slowly, an understanding of how the database system processes SQL statements can help you diagnose and solve the problem.

We start with single-table queries, then multiple-table queries. Finally, we discuss a plan you can follow to improve the performance of your own SQL statements.

Two approaches have been used by relational database systems for access path selection. Historically, the earliest method was based on heuristics – rules that if the query had one of these, then the database system would use some specific method to process it, without considering the contents of the database itself. Later, IBM introduced a cost-based approach, comparing the estimated cost of processing a statement using many different approaches and choosing the method with the lowest cost estimate.[33] Experience has shown that the heuristic method occasionally chose fantastically inefficient strategies, that the cost-based method did not choose. Today, virtually every major database system uses cost-based access path selection.

To estimate the cost of different strategies for processing a query, it's necessary to have some knowledge of the contents of the database. IBM

---

[33] Selinger, Astrahan, Chamberlin, Lorie, Price. Access path selection in a relational database management system. SIGMOD '79: Proceedings of the 1979 ACM SIGMD international conference on management of data, (May 1979) 23-34.

introduced a utility in their systems called RUNSTATS, that gathers statistics about the database. Oracle has a similar utility that is called GATHER_STATS_JOB. These utilities scan the database and collect statistics used to estimate costs of access path selection strategies. The database administrator schedules these utilities. Since they read every row of every table in the database, they take some time to complete. The utility should be run often enough so that major changes in the makeup of the database are reflected, so that good query processing strategies are chosen.

These are some of the statistics gathered by RUNSTATS:

- For each table:
  - Number of rows
  - Number of pages
  - Average row length
- For each column:
  - Cardinality
  - Number of nulls
  - Data distribution
- For each index:
  - Number of leaf pages
  - Levels
  - Branching factor

The optimizer, as it is usually called, selects which indexes to use, chooses the order of using indexes, chooses which join the algorithms to use, and decides when to apply predicates. The parts of a query that are of interest to the optimizer are the FROM clause, that gives the table names, and the WHERE clause, that gives the predicates.

8.2   Single-Table Queries

For a query of a single table, the WHERE clause is the focus of the optimizer. The WHERE clause is made up of conditions, connected by the logical operators AND, OR and NOT. Each condition references a column. Conditions may be equals, not equal to, greater than, less than, not greater than, not less than, range and LIKE.

For all the conditions except LIKE, if there is an index on the column referenced in the condition, then the index can be used to evaluate the condition. LIKE requires a table scan to compare each value with the mask in the LIKE condition.

For example, for SAL > 20, the index for SAL can be searched for the value 20, then all values less than that are matches. For JOB = 'VP', the index for JOB can be searched to find a match for VP.

Now consider this combination of conditions:

SAL > 100 AND JOB = 'VP'

What is the best way to process these conditions? An index can be used to find the rows that meet one of the conditions, and those rows can be retrieved and tested for the other condition. But which index should be used, if there are indexes on both columns?

The best choice would be to use the index that would be likely to produce the smallest number of rows for subsequent processing. In this case, SAL > 100 is likely to produce many candidates. JOB = 'VP' is an exact match on a column that has many different values, so the number of candidates resulting would be small. Clearly, the best choice would be to use the index for JOB to look for a match for VP and then retrieve those rows and check them for SAL > 100.

This is an example of the notion of *selectivity*: an estimate of the fraction of rows of a table that make a predicate true. A smaller value of selectivity is more desirable, because a smaller number of rows will be produced. It's possible to estimate the selectivity of a condition by the operator used and the number of rows in the table. The selectivity of conditions can be combined using rules covering logical operators, to determine which part of the WHERE clause to evaluate using the index. The table below shows some examples:

Form of Predicate	Selectivity
column = value	$1/n$
column != value	$1 - 1/n$ (nearly 1)
column > value	(high value − search value)/(high value − low value)
column like 'value'	N
p1 or p2	$F(p1) + f(p2)$
p1 and p2	$F(p1) * f(p2)$

The last two rows are the rules for combining *and* and *or* conditions. The selectivity of the *and* of two conditions is the product of the selectivities of each condition; the selectivity of the *or* of two conditions is the sum of the selectivity of the two conditions.

Now it is possible to formulate a method for processing single-table queries:

1. Determine which columns referenced in the WHERE clause have indexes
2. Find the selectivity of each of the indexes
3. Estimate the selectivity of each condition
4. Use the most selective index-condition combination to retrieve rows that satisfy that condition
5. Retrieve and examine each row to determine which other conditions are satisfied

8.3   Multi-Table Queries (Joins)

A join is a subset of the Cartesian product of the tables being joined. That is, the result of a join is a subset of all the rows of the first table pasted to all the rows of the second table. If the first table has n rows and the second table has m rows, then the Cartesian product will have mn rows. The figure below shows an example of a Cartesian product:

Table R

employee	payscale
james	1
jones	2
johns	1
smith	2

Table S

payscale	pay
1	10000
2	20000
3	30000

Table Q = R x S

employee	payscale	payscale	pay
james	1	1	10000
james	1	2	20000
james	1	3	30000
jones	2	1	10000
jones	2	2	20000
jones	2	3	30000
johns	1	1	10000
johns	1	2	20000
johns	1	3	30000
smith	2	1	10000
smith	2	2	20000
smith	2	3	30000

Figure 81. Cartesian Product of Tables R and S

Of course, the entire Cartesian product is not of much interest--the joins of interest are all subsets of the Cartesian product. In this case, the most practical subset would appear to be a join of the two tables based on equality of *payscale*, that could be used to make a list of every employee's salary. The query to produce that result would be:

```
SELECT EMPLOYEE, PAY
FROM R, S
WHERE R.PAYSCALE = S.PAYSCALE;
```

A simple algorithm for processing a two-table join would be the following:

1. Form the Cartesian product of the tables involved in the join

2. Scan rows of the Cartesian product, testing each against all the criteria in the WHERE clause

3. Eliminate rows of the Cartesian product that don't meet the conditions

This algorithm would produce correct results, and of course it's easy to implement. However, its performance would be extremely poor, and the Cartesian product produced as an intermediate result would be huge. For example, to join two million-row tables, a Cartesian product of a trillion rows would be produced!

The challenge of processing joins, then, is to find algorithms that produce the same result as the algorithm above that use far fewer resources.

Of course, not all joins involve only two tables. A single join query can include any number of tables. Twelve-table joins are not unusual. In the case of multi-table joins, they are processed two tables at a time. Thus, the same algorithms used for two-table joins are used for multi-table joins. For multi-table joins, though, there is the added question of which join to process first, and in what order to process the joins.

Most joins are equijoins, so this discussion is limited to equijoins. The methods for processing other types of joins closely parallel those for equijoins.

These are the principal algorithms for join processing:

1. Nested-loop join
2. Hash join
3. Sort-merge join
4. Cartesian join

Nested-Loop

The nested-loop method scans the "outer" table, reading the "inner" table once for each row in the outer table, to find matching values. This diagram illustrates:

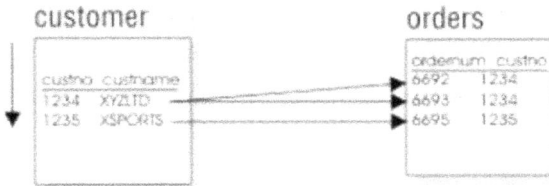

1. Scan outer table.   2. Read inner table once for
                            each row found in outer table.

Figure 82. Nested-Loop

The inner table will be scanned once, while the outer table will be scanned once for every row in the inner table. The table with higher cardinality is chosen as the inner table. The nested-loop method has approximately the same number of operations as the cartesian product. In fact, the Cartesian product is being formed, row by row, but the rest of the conditions are evaluated as the rows of the Cartesian product is formed, so the whole Cartesian product is not stored. If the two tables have m and n rows, the total number of retrievals is $m + m*n$.

The nested-loop algorithm is:

> {For each row r do
> (if r(a) = s(b) then
> concatenate r and s, place in table Q)}

If there is an index on either column, then the table with that column is used as the inner table, because those retrievals will not require a scan. For moderate values of n, the number of equivalent row retrievals needed for an index access is about $2n$, so the number of accesses to process the join is approximately

$$m + 2 * n.$$

Hash Join
A hash function is used to map a range of values occurring in the data into a smaller range of values that corresponds to storage addresses. For example, a hashing algorithm could be used to map numbers from 1 to 100,000,000 into 10,000 addresses.

One method for joining two large tables would be to scan the first table and build a list of all the values in the column to be used for the join. Then the second table is scanned, and the saved values are compared with the values of the join column of the second table, identifying the matching values for the join. However, if there are many rows in the two tables, the intermediate table to be stored could be of prohibitive size.

Hashing can be used to reduce the size of the list of stored values. For example, suppose we have a range of numbers from 1 to 100,000,000, that appears in one column in each of two tables A and B that are to be joined. Suppose the columns are A.X and B.X, and suppose each table has 1,000,000 rows.

This figure shows a fragment of the hash table produced by five values of A.X:

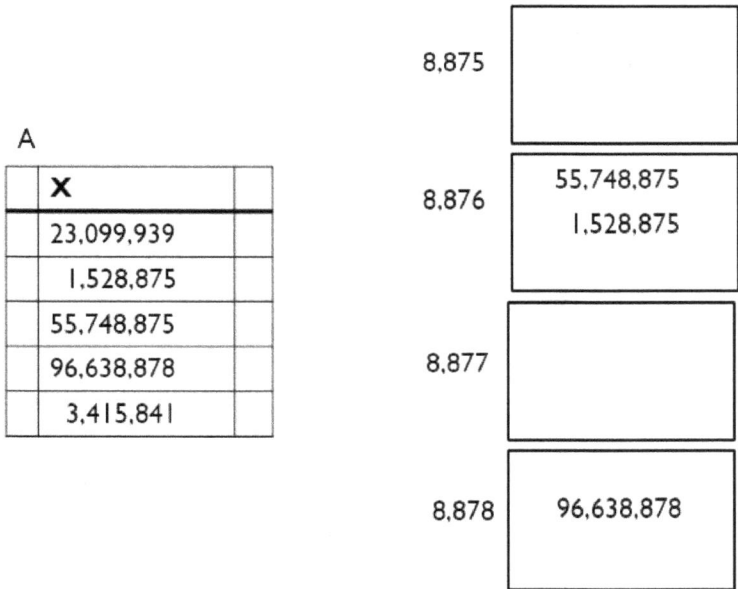

Figure 83. Hash Table Fragment During Pass One

Three of the values shown from the fragment of A.X have hashed into the values shown in the fragment of the hash table. In addition to the value of A.X, the identifier of the row holding the value would be stored so that it can be retrieved as a result of the join. Each "bucket" in the hash table can hold several values of A.X.

Once the hash table has been built during pass one, then pass two begins. This figure shows the processing of pass two, with the same fragment of the hash table:

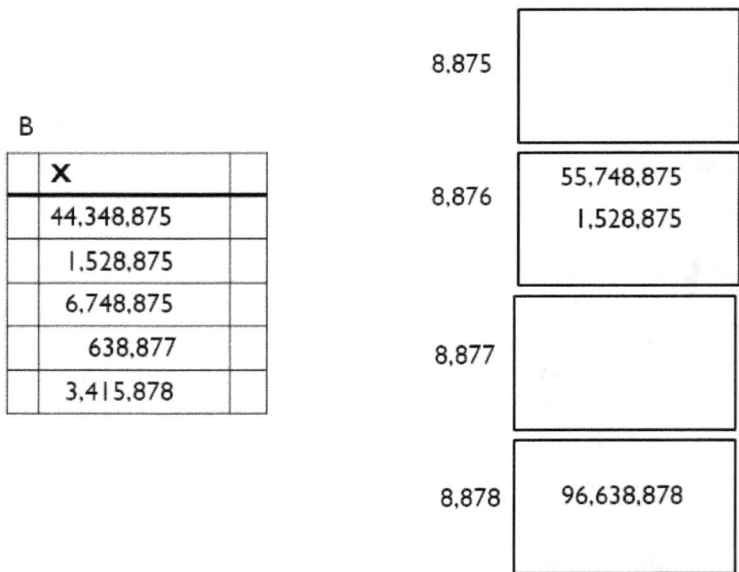

Figure 84. Hash Table Fragment During Pass Two

During the second pass, the hash function is applied to each value of B.X, and the values of A.X stored at that location in the list are examined. If they match, then the two rows are combined and processed as part of the result of the join.

The algorithm can be expressed as follows:

```
for each row r in R do
  {hash on join attributes r(a)
  place tuples in hash table based on hash
values};
for each row s in S do
  {hash on join attributes s(b)
  if s hashes to a nonempty bucket of hash table
for R then
    {if r(a) matches any s(b) in bucket,
    concatenate r and s
    place in table Q}}
```

On the first pass, a hash table is built by applying a hash function to the join column of the first table, building a list of up to 10,000 hash values of the row identifiers for rows that have a value that hashes to that value. On the second pass, the second table is scanned, each value of the join column is hashed, and the hash value is looked up in the hash table. If a match is found, then the rows with values that hashed to the same value are all fetched, and the values of the hash columns are compared.

A popular hashing algorithm is to divide the original value by a prime number and take the remainder as the hashed value. A comparative study of different hashing algorithms conducted by IBM Research at the Almaden Research Center[34] showed that this

---

[34] Lum, Vincent Y., Yuen, P. S. T. and Dodd, M. Key-to-Address Techniques: A Fundamental Performance Study on

hashing function can be used on a wide variety of different types of values and provides very good performance.

Merge Join

The merge join is very efficient when the two tables are ordered by the join columns. With one pass through both tables, all the matching values can be identified. If the two tables have m and n rows, then only $m + n$ rows need to be fetched

Usually, though, the tables are not stored in join order, so they must first be sorted. After the tables are sorted, then the number of row fetches is simply $n + m$, the sum of the number of rows in both tables. The algorithm for the merge join is:

> Stage 1: Sort
> Sort A on A.X
> Sort B on B.X
> Stage 2: Merge
> Read first row from A;
> Read first row from B
> For each row of A do:
>   {while A.X < B.X
>   Read next row from A;
>   If A.X = B.X then
>   Join A and B
>   Place in output table};

Large Existing Formatted Files. *Communications of the ACM* 14, 4 (April 1971), pp. 228-239.

Note that if there is an index on the join column of
one of the tables, then this algorithm becomes the
same as nested-loop, with the indexed table as the
inner table.

Cartesian Join
The Cartesian join produces the Cartesian product as
the result. Every row of the first table is appended to
every row of the second table. If one table has n rows
and the other has m rows, the Cartesian product will
have m*n rows. Processing of this join is
straightforward, if lengthy.

Indexes
An index on a join column greatly improves
performance of the join. Frequently, if there are
performance problems with joins, simply creating an
index can resolve the problems. Note that an index
carries some costs with it, because the index must be
updated when changes are made to the column that it
indexes. In addition, the change process must be
protected from concurrency problems by locking the
portions of the index that have been changed until the
transaction commits.

Multi-Table Joins
A multi-table join is processed two tables at a time.
The order of processing joins must be selected, as
well as the method for each join.

The criterion generally used to decide the order of
processing joins is to begin by processing the join
that is expected to produce the fewest rows in its
result, so that the processing of the next join in the

sequence will begin with as few rows as possible. All the joins are processed in order of expected size of result, with the join expected to produce the largest result processed last.

Once the order of processing is decided, then the same criteria used to choose processing strategies for two-table joins are used for each join.

Summary
This has been an overview of how queries are processed, intended to provide a starting point for understanding the performance tradeoffs a particular system that you work with.

8.4 Your Performance Cookbook
Technical book publishers provide fat books about performance of commercial database systems. These books provide details about the myriad options that are provided for use by database administrators to tune performance. If you're having performance problems with your application, don't buy one of these books as your first step. There are several useful steps you can take before you need the big book! They are laid out here.

Often, performance issues arise from how the database, and SQL, are being used in the application. Here are the recommended steps to follow:

1. Examine the program
2. Look at SQL in the program
3. Look at indexes
4. Test
5. Use EXPLAIN PLAN

6.   Beyond EXPLAIN

Examine the Program
Some performance problems are caused by gross misuse of the database system. This won't be the case for your own program, but if you're helping a colleague, first ask what the program is doing and examine the program. Programmers who have no database experience will often ask a neighbor how to retrieve from the database, and simply copy code without understanding what it is doing.

This first check is to consider what's being done in program logic and what's being done in SQL. For example, SQL may be used to retrieve rows one and a time and then the program sorts them; in that case, of course, ORDER BY in the query saves programming effort as well as speeding up the operation.

Look at SQL
Now examine the use of SQL. Has the most effective use been made of the features of SQL? Programmers who don't know SQL may not know about GROUP BY, or HAVING within GROUP BY, or arithmetic operations in the SELECT clause. Give the SQL a careful review.

Look at Indexes
If a table has fewer than 1,000 rows, it's likely that the database system will do a physical scan of the table even if there are indexes. But for tables with greater than 1,000 rows, pay attention to any columns that are referenced in the WHERE clause. Is there an

index on these columns? If two tables are joined and neither table has an index on the join columns, the database system has no option but to perform $n * m$ operations, while a single index reduces it to approximately $n + m$ operations.

Most of the performance problems that application programmers experience are solved with indexes.

Test and Analyze

Test the program for performance to determine where the bottlenecks are. It's always possible for the programmer to have misunderstood where the performance issues are with the program. A simple way to check the performance of SQL statements is to run them online without the program and time them. This method can establish whether the performance issues relate to database use or not, and which SQL statements are causing the problem.

Use EXPLAIN PLAN

IBM invented the EXPLAIN utility, that shows the processing strategy for each WHERE clause. For queries that appear to be bottlenecks, run it, and in the result, look for table scans, Cartesian product joins and the like.

Once you've understood the database system's strategy for processing the query, you can consider additional indexes or other physical database changes to improve performance.

The figure below gives an example of an EXPLAIN PLAN for Oracle. You'll see that the result of the EXPLAIN PLAN is stored in PLAN_TABLE:

```
EXPLAIN PLAN
    SET STATEMENT_ID = 'Raise in Tokyo'
    INTO plan_table
    FOR UPDATE employees
        SET salary = salary * 1.10
        WHERE department_id =
            (SELECT department_id FROM departments
                WHERE location_id = 1200);

SELECT LPAD(' ',2*(LEVEL-1))||operation operation, options,
    object_name, position
    FROM plan_table
    START WITH id = 0 AND statement_id = 'Raise in Tokyo'
    CONNECT BY PRIOR id = parent_id AND statement_id = 'Raise in Tokyo'
    ORDER BY operation, options, object_name, position;
```

OPERATION	OPTIONS	OBJECT_NAME	POSITION
UPDATE STATEMENT			2
UPDATE		EMPLOYEES	1
TABLE ACCESS	FULL	EMPLOYEES	1
VIEW		index$_join$_00	1
		2	
HASH JOIN			1
INDEX	RANGE SCAN	DEPT_LOCATION_I	1
		X	
INDEX	FAST FULL SCAN	DEPT_ID_PK	2

Figure 85. EXPLAIN PLAN

Beyond EXPLAIN PLAN

Every commercial database system provides many performance options, often dealing with physical storage of data. The relational approach requires that data be viewed as a set of independent tables, but it does not require that the data be stored in that fashion. For example, if two tables are commonly joined together, most database systems allow for the rows of those two tables to be stored in the same page if they share a value of a join column. This allows for rapid processing of joins of those two tables, without the need to denormalize the data model.

It's important to make a full exploration of the performance options the database system offers before considering denormalization.

Denormalization can lead to much more complex programming and difficult future maintenance of the application. More important, though, using features of the database system that are already available is easy to do as well as effective.

Chapter 9   Database in the Enterprise

9.1   Introduction

This book is about the database approach, that an enterprise can store its data in an integrated collection that uses integrity constraints based on interrelationships to improve quality of the data. As more and more of the enterprise's data is added to the database, the quality of data improves. Also, the development of a robust data model, that does not change significantly while the processes that access it change over time, produce considerable reductions in the cost and effort needed for software maintenance. There is a classic paper from the Harvard Business Review that talks about how the centralization of data can help make the IT department more effective, by freeing up programmers to work on new systems, instead of spending all their time on maintenance of old systems. While the technology described in the paper is obsolete, the basic ideas are still pertinent.[35]

Unfortunately, the widespread use of relational database systems has not led to such a state of nirvana; in fact, the promise of a single, integrated collection of an enterprise's data is not realized in most organizations. This chapter is intended to portray a view of the actual situation in many organizations.

---

[35] C. F. Gibson and R. L. Nolan. Managing the four states of EDP growth. *Harvard Business review* 52, 1 (January-February 1974).

These trends can be seen in many large organizations today:

- Process-centric rather than data-centric programming
- Agile data modeling to accompany agile programming
- Multiple databases and associated confusion

9.2   Data-centric vs process-centric

In the data-centric approach to programming, first a robust, normalized data model is developed. In addition to normalization, following Roberts's Rules Three and Four add additional value to the data model. Such a data model will not incorporate any elements of the business processes that are being implemented.

Programming begins once the data model is established. Certainly, as the effort progresses more is learned about the data, and there may be some changes to the data model, but they will be minimal.

If a process-centric approach is used instead, the focus is on programming rather than data. Instead of experienced data modelers to develop the data model, it's left to programmers without specialized training or experience. The data model may even be developed in parallel with programming.

A result is eventually produced with the process-centric approach, but at considerable cost, because of the rework of many programs that takes place when changes are made to the data model after programming work is under way.

The result produced by the process-centric approach is inferior to the result of the data-centric approach because the final data model may suffer from lack of normalization or may incorporate process elements that may introduce added complexity when business processes change, and programs must be altered.

9.3   Agile Development

Agile development is a replacement for the rigid software development approaches of the past, that featured large amounts of documentation and a rigid development plan from the outset.

The space program was successful in using what's called the "waterfall" approach. Programming was divided into phases, such as analysis, design, implementation, and testing. Once each phase was completed, the next phase began, and work in the previous phase could not be changed—like going over a waterfall.

Unfortunately, space missions are very different from on-the-earth business processes. With a space mission, the requirements for software can be fixed at the start and held constant during the development. For earthly software development, the requirements for the software are constantly changing due to changes in regulations, competition in the marketplace and other factors.

The agile approach emphasizes making parts of the software work incrementally in small teams, working with customer representatives as work progresses and welcoming changes in requirements. This is intended to permit a development project to keep abreast of changes in requirements as the project progresses. The emphasis is on producing working code, rather than lots of documents.

The leaders of the agile movement are skilled programmers, not skilled data modelers. Many of them don't understand normalization (much less Roberts's Rules!) or its importance. They likely do not understand the importance of keeping process artifacts out of data models.

I've heard one of them state that because ALTER TABLE permits a table to be changed after the database is created, there's no need to be concerned about making changes to the data model during the development effort.

The Agile approach has much to recommend it. Short "sprints" of development to meet small goals can be very productive. Involving customers in requirements as the effort progresses, instead of only at the end, is a great idea. However, not paying attention to the data model at the outset is a mistake that can bring huge penalties later.

A compromise approach would be to focus data modeling on the entity types involved in the first sprint and complete the modeling of those entity types before programming begins. There is some risk in programming before the entire data model is complete, but the principles of normalization are helpful in producing a sound data model even if all the entity types haven't been analyzed.

Using this approach, it's possible to keep the data modeling effort ahead of programming, so that every sprint has a robust data model to use as a foundation for software development.

9.4   Promise of the Database Approach
The promise of the database is a single collection of all an enterprise's data, all interrelated, using these relationships to implement constraints that continually improve the quality of the data collection as more topics are added to the database.

This ideal enterprise situation would like something like this:

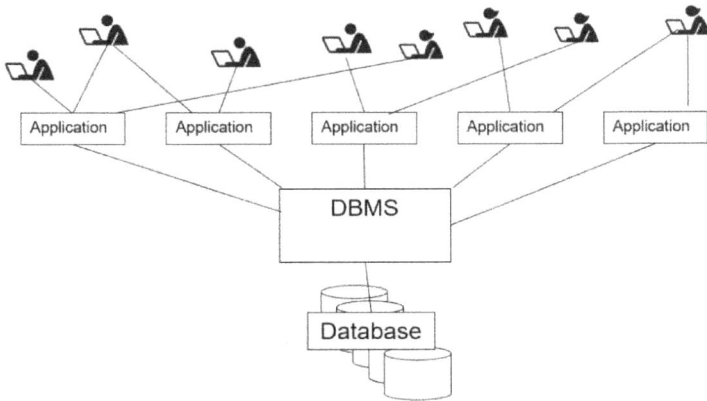

Figure 86. Ideal Enterprise Use of DBMS

This is the use of the enterprise database as the "single source of truth" for data. Each fact is represented just once, and it's protected from software and hardware failures. Unfortunately, this "data nirvana" is not often achieved.

More often, a sizable enterprise has multiple databases, each supporting multiple applications. The situation might look like this; but there can be many more than just two databases:

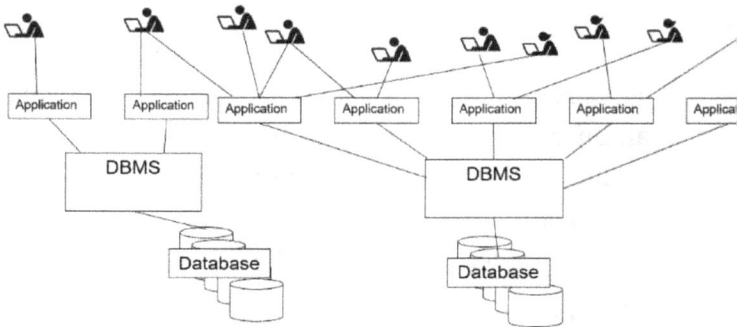

Figure 87. Enterprise with Multiple Databases

How does this situation develop? A new important application might be acquired--such as payroll or inventory or human resources—that won't work with the enterprise database. The acquired application might require its own database. Or a company might be acquired, along with all its IT infrastructure. Instead of redeveloping all the applications of the acquired company, the decision is made to continue using them along with the acquiror's applications. This happens frequently in the banking industry, where acquisitions are very common. Large banks commonly run many systems from acquired banks, that provide services to that bank's customers.

The result of this phenomenon is what's called data
silos—distinct data reservoirs that don't share data
easily, like grain silos that we see around farms:

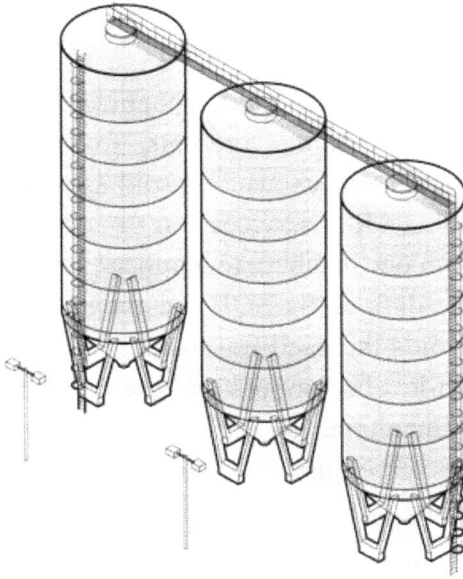

Figure 88. Silos

The result is data chaos! One way to deal with the
problem is to write programs to transfer data between
databases. Commonly, these transfers are made
during times of relative inactivity, with potentially
many programs running every night. Data failures
indicate an error that must be addressed, usually
requiring the intervention of a person, that may
become very labor-intensive. One major bank runs

more than 10,000 different program executions to copy data between databases every day.

When applications are changed, then the data transfer programs must be changed as well, and tested, and the release of the new transfer programs must be coordinated with application updates.

The database vendors recognized the business opportunity that this presents, so they introduced replication services, usually sold as a database add-on product. Rep services can be scheduled to copy data from one database to another. The transfers can often be defined by SQL statements on both sides. This avoids the need for custom programming, and the high-level setup makes these transfers relatively easy to maintain. Nevertheless, if there are a lot of transfers, the use of multiple databases adds significant cost to the enterprise.

If many executions of rep services are run each day, some overall discipline is needed to organize these transfers. Some structure must be introduced into a mass of transfers that can look like this:

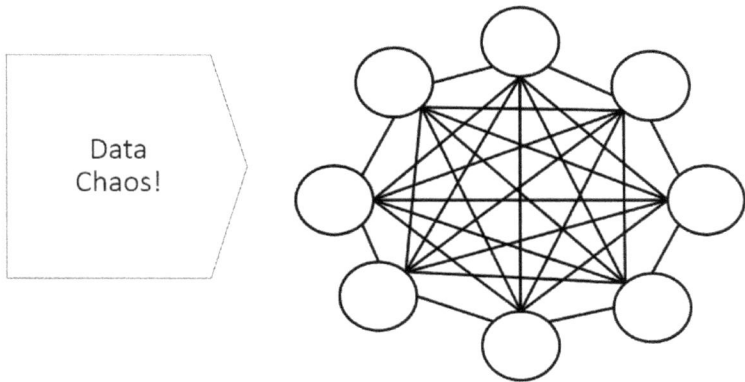

Figure 89. Uncontrolled Data Transfers

It's easy to see that without some discipline, with multiple copies of data, errors can exist and even propagate through multiple transfers.

9.5   Master Data Management
A discipline has evolved to identify some data as *master* and some as *slave,* arranging storage accordingly.   This discipline is called master data management. Master data is identified and stored in a separate repository. Then changes to master data are copied into the hub, then copied outward from the hub.

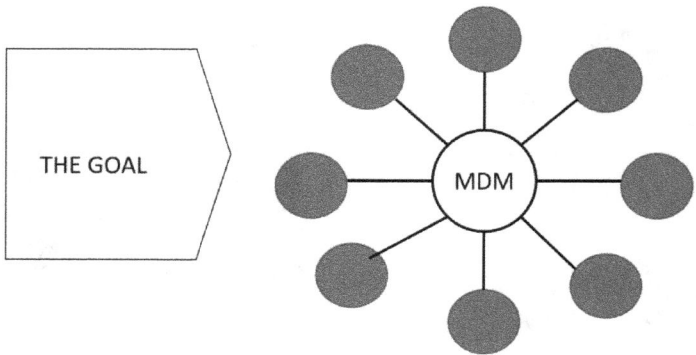

Figure 90. Master Data Management

Master data is defined as the consistent, uniform set of identifiers and attributes that describe the core entities of the enterprise, such as customers, prospects, citizens, suppliers, hierarchies, products, and charts of account. Master data is generally broken down into several main categories:

- *Master data* is the people, places and things involved in an organization's business. They tend to be nouns. In database terms, they are entity types that are important to the organization.

- *Transactional data* describes business events, such as sales, patient visits, repairs completed. Transaction data tends to be verbs.

- *Reference data* is sets of values or classification schemes that are referred to by systems, applications, processes, and reports.

- *Reporting data* is organized for reporting and business intelligence.

Master data is about the business entities that provide context for business transactions. Frequent categories are:

- Parties (individuals and organizations) and their roles
  - Customers
  - Patients
  - Students
  - Employees
- Products
- Financial Structures

Master data is generally concerned with business entities, and not transactions.

Transactional data describes events—that is, the change resulting from a transaction, and is usually described with verbs. Transaction data always has a time dimension, a numerical value and refers to one of more objects that are reference data. Some examples are:

- Financial:
  - Orders, invoices, payments
- Work:
  - Plans, activity records
- Logistics:
  - Deliveries, storage records, travel records

Reference data is used to classify or categorize other data. Some examples are:

- Units of measurement

- Country codes
- Fixed conversion rates

Changes to reference data may involve changes to business processes; for example, adding a new customer type entails a change in business process to manage that new customer type.

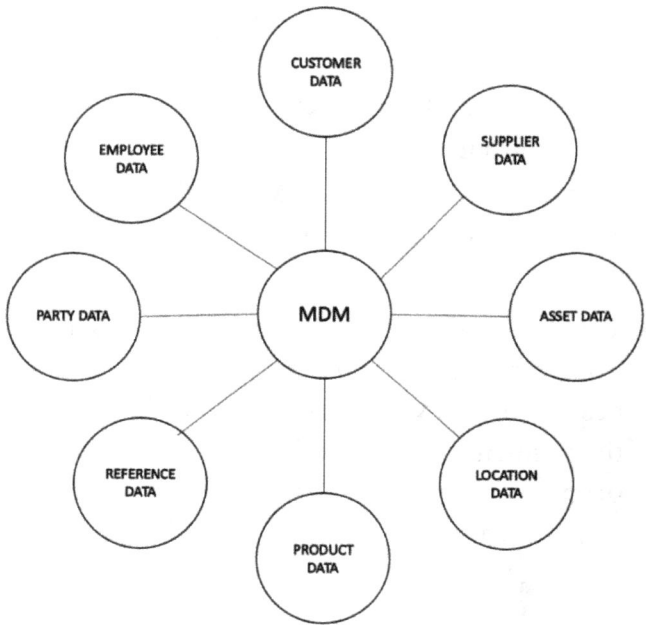

Figure 91. Master Data Organized by Master Data Hub

There are several products that are called master data hubs. They are used to store master data and provide to all the applications and databases that need copies.

Master Data Management Today

Many companies have produced products to support master data management. However, there is growing realization that the need for data rationalization within an enterprise goes beyond just the structured data processed by relational database systems and includes repositories of text data and data from social media as well. There is a movement toward the cataloging and integration of all an organization's data resources. This is well expressed by the Data-Centric Manifesto:

We have uncovered a root cause of the messy state of Information Architecture in large institutions today. It is the prevailing application-centric mindset that gives applications priority over data. The remedy is to flip this on its head. Data is the center of the universe; applications are ephemeral.

These are the key principles of the data centric manifesto[36]:

- *Data is a key asset of any organization.*
- *Data is self-describing and does not rely on an application for interpretation and meaning.*
- *Data is expressed in open, non-proprietary formats.*
- *Access to and security of the data is a responsibility of the data layer, and not managed by applications.*
- *Applications are allowed to visit the data, perform their magic and express the results of their process back into the data layer for all to share.*

---

[36] Datacentricmanifesto.org

Data-centric is a major departure from the current application-centric approach to systems development and management. Migration to the data-centric approach will not happen by itself. It needs champions.

Leadership Opportunities

Today there is increasing realization that leveraging an organization's data assets are key to its success. However, especially in larger organizations, the data resources are in disarray. The people who solve these problems for large organizations will have continued, lengthy employment, and the opportunity make important contributions, with the recognition that goes with it.

About the Author
Dave Roberts holds the BS degree in EE from Johns Hopkins, MS in EE from the University of Pennsylvania, and the MS in Computer Science from the University of Maryland College Park.

His 40-year career has spanned many different positions dealing with database management systems, giving him unique perspectives to write this textbook.

He was employee #12 at Oracle, where he established the Eastern Region. He then joined a large organization that is a developer of database applications. He headed an internal group that supported database systems used by the organization. Later he served as CTO for a part of that organization that developed large-scale applications that used database systems. Finally, he served as Enterprise Data Architect in that organization. During this entire time, he taught graduate courses at George Washington University on database management.

Drawing on Dave's unique experience, this book focuses on the skills needed to develop database applications, with emphasis on topics that are generally not well understood by students who complete graduate database courses.

www.ingramcontent.com/pod-product-compliance
Lightning Source LLC
Chambersburg PA
CBHW050636190326
41458CB00008B/2300